SIMULATORS

SIMULATORS

BY NORMAN F. SMITH
AND DOUGLAS W. SMITH

FRANKLIN WATTS
NEW YORK • LONDON • TORONTO • SYDNEY
A VENTURE BOOK • 1989

Diagrams by Richard Leyden

Photographs courtesy of:
Delta Airlines, Inc.: pp. 10, 44; The Singer Company:
pp. 22, 27, 35, 36, 46, 61, 63, 66, 69, 110, 112;
Federal Aviation Agency: p. 41 (top); The Smithsonian
Institution: p. 41 (bottom); NASA: pp. 74, 78, 79, 81, 83;
Maritime Institute of Technology: pp. 95, 99, 101, 104

Library of Congress Cataloging-in-Publication Data

Smith, Norman F.
Simulators

(A Venture book)
Includes index.
Summary: Discusses the invention and operation
of simulators, how they are used to train people for
responsible positions in aviation, transportation,
the military, and spaceflight, and their possible
use in the future.
1. Synthetic training devices—Juvenile literature.
[1. Synthetic training devices] I. Smith, Douglas W.,
1949-   II. Title. III. Series: Venture book
(Franklin Watts, Inc.)
T65.5.S9S65 1989   620'.0078   89-9083
ISBN 0-531-10812-0

FOR RACHEL,
HANS, AND
  CORBIN SMITH

CONTENTS

SIMULATORS

Cockpit of a modern airliner

PREFACE
MACHINES THAT PRETEND

The airline pilot faces a maze of instruments, switches, and controls, which he must use to maneuver his airplane speedily and precisely, even under the stress of dire emergencies.

A nuclear power plant operator has enormous power at his fingertips. Although he is aided by automatic controls and backup systems, he still must be trained to operate safely a huge, complicated panel of switches, gauges, and controls.

An oil refinery operator controls from a complex nerve center acres of tangled pipes, valves, and processing equipment containing highly flammable liquids.

Railroad engineers and ship captains are responsible for the operation of vehicles of great power and enormous weight, which they must have under full, safe control at all times.

Training for highly responsible positions of these kinds used to be performed almost entirely "on the job." There were obvious dangers in practicing flying an airliner with one engine out, even with no passengers aboard. There would be danger in poking around in a fog while training a student commander on the bridge of an ocean ship, or in practicing "scram" shutdowns in a real nuclear plant.

The simulator was born many decades ago in the mind of an aviator whose vision was far ahead of his time. After an uncertain start as an amusement-park device, the airplane simulator was quickly brought into widespread practical use by the disaster that occurred in 1934 when the U.S. Army Air Corps took on the task of flying the nation's mail in all kinds of weather without adequate training. Over the course of a few days, five pilots were killed.

Simulators were first employed to train pilots for the single task of flying by instruments. The simulation concept then spread rapidly. First adapted to military use, it then was applied to other forms of transportation and to industry.

This book tells the story of the invention of the simulator. It also explains how simulators work; how they are used to train people for responsible positions in aviation, transportation, industry, the military, and spaceflight; and how they may affect our world, now and in the future.

ONE

A FLIGHT TO NOWHERE

No one could have guessed what was in store for Flight 234 as the airliner taxied out for takeoff. The captain, a balding man in his mid-fifties, steered the Boeing jet with the small wheel at his left. The first officer (known also as the copilot), a younger man with half as many as the captain's thirty-odd years of flight experience, worked his hands up and down the panels of switches and gauges overhead and on the forward panel, checking the aircraft's systems once more. The second officer (or flight engineer) in the sideways-facing seat at the flight-engineer panel, shuffled his flight paperwork aside and readied the switches on his panel, reading from the taxi checklist he held in his hand.

"Before-takeoff checklist," called the captain.

The flight engineer swung his chair into a forward-facing position and read, "Flight attendants."

"Notified and acknowledged," responded the first officer.

"Antiskid switches?"

"On."

"Continuous ignition?"

"Checked: on."

"Navigation lights?"

"On."

"Altimeter, flight, navigation instruments."

All eyes scanned the instruments in this last-minute effort to detect any abnormalities.

"Set and cross-checked," came the response to each item.

"Flaps?"

"Set for takeoff," confirmed the first officer.

Checklist completed, the big jet was cleared into takeoff position. The tension in the cockpit rose as the aircraft turned down the dark runway marked only by the lights outlining its edges that ended abruptly about 2 miles away.

Takeoff and landing are the two most stressful and dangerous events in an airplane flight. Peak performance is demanded of all the major systems during takeoff, including the engines, flight controls, wings, flaps, hydraulic systems—and the pilots—to get the airplane safely into the air, out of airport traffic, and on the way to its destination. Despite all care taken, no one can predict what failures may lurk in the machinery, ready to spring up at the most inopportune time. The pilot team in the cockpit must closely monitor the aircraft's instruments and be ready in an instant for any emergency, or series of emergencies, no matter how unlikely.

A voice crackled over the cockpit radio speakers: "Flight two thirty-four, maintain runway heading after departure; cleared for takeoff."

The first officer pressed his microphone button and said, "Flight two thirty-four, Roger."

As the captain pushed the throttles forward, the bank of engine instruments came to life, with needles and counters showing vital information such as fuel flow, engine pressures, temperatures, and engine speed. The acceleration pushed the three pilots back into their seats as the aircraft began to rumble down the runway. The lights at the edge of the runway sped past the cockpit side windows with increasing speed.

"V-one, rotate," called the copilot when the airspeed indicator showed the speed at which the pilot should begin to lift the aircraft's nose from the runway.

"V-two," he announced a few seconds later, when the minimum safe climbing speed had been reached and the aircraft could leave the ground. The captain raised the nose a bit higher and the rumble of the wheels on the pavement suddenly stopped. The jet was airborne.

"Positive rate of climb," announced the copilot.

"Landing gear up!" commanded the captain. The rumble of the landing gear folding into the belly of the aircraft suddenly went silent when the gear doors closed a few seconds later.

As the airplane climbed toward its cruising altitude, the bright lights of the airport dropped away, and soon only the twinkling lights of the nearby city could be seen on the horizon. Suddenly these lights winked out as the jet ascended into the cloud deck above. The 80-ton machine seemed from the cockpit to slip quietly upward through an empty night sky.

Suddenly a loud bell shattered the quiet of the cockpit and a bright red light on the forward panel caught every eye.

"Engine fire!" bellowed the copilot. "Number two engine."

With quick motions, the captain pulled back the throttle on that engine, cut off the fuel, and pulled the fire handle to activate the fire extinguisher system.

"Engine-fire checklist," called the captain, as he trimmed the aircraft's flight controls and rechecked the engine instruments, which now showed shutdown of one of the three engines. "Call the control tower and tell them we have a problem and would like to level off here for a while, and that we'll be coming back into the airport."

"Ready with the engine-fire checklist, captain," said the flight engineer.

"Read it!"

To each item on the checklist the copilot responded, flipping switches and checking instruments to determine the status of the impaired aircraft.

"Captain, the engine fire has been extinguished, and all the appropriate checklists are completed," the flight engineer announced. The crew's next task was to review the various systems of the aircraft that would be inoperative for the remainder of the flight.

Suddenly the aircraft broke out above the clouds into a clear and starlit black sky, at which time the moderate turbulence they had been experiencing also ended.

"Captain, I have some more bad news for you," said the flight engineer. "We appear to be losing hydraulic fluid."

"Understand. Keep an eye on it."

"Uh-oh," called the flight engineer. "It's draining fast now. I think we might lose it all!"

As if the loss of an engine was not enough, the flight crew would face a whole new set of problems if one of the aircraft's hydraulic systems were to go out of business. Hydraulic systems normally operate the flight controls of the aircraft, raise and lower the landing gear, operate brakes and ground steering. Because the airliner was built with backup systems, a loss of one of its primary systems would almost never be a serious problem. However, it meant an even bigger workload for an already busy flight-deck crew. The uncertainty of how the aircraft would now handle also added to the pressure on the crew, and made it urgent to land the crippled aircraft as soon as possible.

"Hydraulic-system-loss checklist," requested the captain, and from his decades of training and experience, he briefed his crew on the highlights of the procedure before beginning the actual checklist.

"We'll have to use abnormal flap settings for landing, and you'll have to crank our landing gear down by hand. Call the control tower and request that towing equipment be standing by after touchdown, because we may be unable to steer off the runway without hydraulic power," said the captain. The flight engineer was flipping through the huge operational manual for the procedures to be used when hydraulic power is lost.

Suddenly the aircraft began to lurch from side to side, and the captain struggled to maintain control.

"I apparently also have some kind of a problem with my roll-axis flight controls—either ailerons or spoilers," he said. Beads of sweat appeared on his brow. "Probably something's broken or jammed, which is why the hydraulic fluid was lost. Nothing we can do about it up here, but I'll sure have my hands full just flying this aircraft. You two complete all the emergency checklists—and let's get this machine back on the ground!"

As each checklist was read, every switch and light, every lever and control was double-checked. The three busy flight-crew members knew what they were up against with their multiply handicapped aircraft. What they did *not* need was another surprise failure—but one was close behind.

Over the radio loudspeaker came news that the "marginal" weather at the airport to which they were now returning had grown worse. Also, the primary instrument-landing system had been knocked out by an electrical storm, leaving only a backup landing system not nearly as precise as the regular system. In addition to everything else that had happened so far, the flight crew now had to prepare for an uncommon type of instrument approach. The deteriorating weather conditions meant they must fly the crippled aircraft through the approach procedure as carefully and precisely as they could to ensure successful sighting of the runway in time for a landing. As they prepared for this final ordeal, lightning flickered occasionally outside the cockpit.

After working hard at the flight controls for nearly a quarter of an hour, the captain said "Let's all review this approach chart." The approach procedure charts were reviewed, and the minimum descent altitudes, final approach compass headings, and elapsed times for the instrument descent were all memorized. More switches and circuit breakers were operated to shut down unneeded systems and activate needed equipment.

"All abnormal and emergency checklists complete," said the flight engineer. "Standing by for landing-gear extension and final landing checklist."

The stars and occasional lightning flashes visible through the cockpit windshield disappeared suddenly as the big jet descended into the cloud layer to begin its instrument-landing approach. Turbulence in the clouds shook the cockpit. The three crew members now concentrated on the flight instruments that would guide them to the runway, continuing their call-outs while monitoring the progress of the approach solely by their instruments.

"Landing gear down," the captain commanded. In a flash the flight engineer was on his hands and knees on the cockpit floor furiously cranking the heavy landing gear down from its cavity in the belly of the aircraft. When the hydraulic system is operating normally, the landing gear is lowered by the flip of a single lever. The loss of that system, however, now made necessary some eight to ten turns of the crank for each of the three wheels.

"Landing gear is down and we have three green lights," called the copilot. This meant that the gear was now locked down and ready for landing. The flight engineer swung back into his seat, refastened his shoulder harness and announced, "Landing checklist now complete."

Their instruments told them that they were on the proper flight path and descent rate to the end of the runway. There were only two questions now: Would they be able to see the runway from the minimum altitude to which they could safely descend, and line up with it in time to make a landing? If not, would they be able to put power on and climb out for another try?

"We're five hundred feet above our minimum descent altitude," said the copilot calmly, dividing his attention between peering at the instruments and out the windshield. "Still no ground contact."

The captain's eyes never left the cockpit flight instruments in front of him. There was no point in looking out anyway, because there was nothing outside to look at but the gray murk of solid clouds.

"Two hundred feet above minimums."

"One hundred feet. I have some ground lights in sight. Still no runway visible."

The captain's right hand tightened on the throttles, ready to push them to maximum thrust if a "missed approach" and climb-out were necessary.

"Minimum descent altitude, approach lights in sight!" called the first officer joyously. At this call, the captain's eyes left the panel instruments to look through the windshield for the touchdown. Several more warning lights blinked on the panel to warn the crew of their close proximity to the ground. This was the point at which the crew had to make that split-second decision—whether to make the landing or climb out for another try.

But the crippled aircraft was lined up with the runway, and the runway lights were soon flashing past under the two wing tips. As the captain eased the throttles closed and drew the wheel back, a firm but welcome jolt rocked the cockpit. The aircraft was on the middle of the dark, wet runway, rolling at 140 miles per hour.

The captain pulled the thrust levers into reverse, and the craft's speed quickly diminished, forcing the crew forward against their shoulder harnesses. As the captain coaxed the ailing hydraulic system to turn the airplane off the runway and onto the taxiway, the flight engineer broke the silence.

"Fire!" he called. "The auxiliary power unit is giving an 'on fire' indication, and I can't put it out with the extinguishing system!"

The crew, already weary from their long bout with one malfunction after another, snapped back to business once again. Braking the aircraft to a stop, the captain roared:

"Passenger-evacuation checklist. Notify the tower to get the fire trucks over here, and get the crew on stations for evacuation!"

The flight engineer grabbed the emergency checklist once again and was shouting his way through it when a new voice from the rear of the cockpit suddenly interrupted.

"That's all for now, fellows. Good job. Let's take a coffee break and talk about it all."

The three weary flight-crew members unfastened their harnesses, climbed out of their seats, and filed slowly through the cockpit door. There was no airliner cabin full of passengers beyond the door, but only a flight of stairs leading down to the computer room below.

The hair-raising flight that the crew had just completed was not a real flight at all. There was no real engine fire, no hydraulic loss, no flight-control malfunctions, no bad weather, no slippery wet runways, no emergency evacuation, no real danger to crew or passengers.

This entire "flight" took place in a stationary, electronic, computerized simulator, often called "the box," located in a modern office building miles from any airport or airplane. All of the problems—the fires, failures, flight-control abnormalities, and poor weather conditions—were simulated by highly sophisticated computers connected to a complete working mock-up that is an exact replica of an aircraft's cockpit. The foggy weather, the stars, the approach and runway lights— real as they appeared—were all computer-generated images projected outside the cockpit windshield. All the emergencies and malfunctions had been invented and imposed by the simulator instructor, who sat quietly

Exterior view of cockpit simulator

at his own "computer-input station" in the rear of the cockpit.

In a lifetime of flying, not many flight crews will encounter such a terrifying sequence of malfunctions and misfortunes. But all flight crews, even very experienced ones, must be exposed to such emergencies and trained to deal with them and to bring the aircraft back down safely.

Performing such training in a real airplane would be expensive and dangerous, if indeed it could be done at all. In a simulator it is safe, easy, and relatively inexpensive. The simulator instructor can program the kind of experiences that he thinks his students need, as well as those required by federal law for pilot certification. After the flight, they can talk over their experience and performance, and if necessary return to the simulator again to repeat the exercise. Aviation simulators have been so successful that they are used today for most of the complex training and periodic checks that are given to airline and military pilots the world over.

In the following chapters we will trace the development of the aviation simulator, which came into use in the 1930s, and examine some other kinds of specialized simulators that are now used to train personnel in aviation, the maritime industry, the railroads, refineries, chemical plants, nuclear power stations, and many other industries.

TWO

DRIVER-TRAINING SIMULATORS

"Start engine."

A dozen students fumble with a dozen starter keys, and the instruments on the dashboards in front of them spring to life.

"Release brake!" called the instructor.

The "thunk!" of released brake levers clatters through the room.

"Signal left turn, and slowly pull away from the curb."

Still fumbling with his brake lever, one student stares straight ahead at the motion-picture screen at the front of the room and forgets to turn his wheel. It doesn't matter—the view on the screen gives each student the feeling that his or her "car" has swung away from the curb and turned into traffic in the right-hand lane. The student grabs his wheel and begins to steer.

"At the next intersection, turn left. Signal left turn now."

Twelve wheels turn cautiously to the left as the "windshield view" on the screen sweeps slowly around the corner. From the distance another car approaches, then whizzes by on the left. A sign reading SPEED LIMIT 35 appears to the right of the roadway. A pedestrian crosses the street at the intersection ahead. A small truck passes from behind.

After a few more intersections, the drivers are turning their steering wheels in unison, eyes on the windshield view on the screen. Then comes the command, "Pull over to the curb and stop engines." The view on the screen moves to the curb and stops.

The instructor looked up from the lights and counters on his control panel. "All right," he said, "now let's review what each of you did right and wrong."

For some students in this class, their first session in the driver-training simulator was a bit elementary. They knew about cars and gearshifts and turn signals. Some had already driven cars or operated tractors on the farm. But for many of the students, this class gave them their first time "behind the wheel."

The "cars" in the simulator are arranged in two rows in the classroom. Each is an exact replica of the driver's station in an automobile. The comfortable bucket seat is adjustable, just like a car seat. The wheel, gearshift, turn signals, and foot pedals all work, as do the instruments on the dashboard. They don't do what controls in a real car do, but they do *something*.

Imagine yourself in the driver's seat. After you properly "start" the "motor," the oil-pressure gauge and the battery-charge indicators on the panel come to life. When you engage the gearshift (or automatic transmission), the car can be "driven." When you press down the accelerator, the speedometer moves up to the speed that a car would have for that amount of pedal depression. When you let up on the accelerator, the car slows down. If you press the brake pedal, the car slows more quickly, depending upon how hard you press.

The motion picture on the screen on the front wall of the classroom shows a windshield view from a car starting, turning, driving, and stopping on the highway. It is not affected, of course, by your actions as the "driver." Everyone in the simulator sees the same scene, roughly a driver's-eye view of each maneuver as it would look if correctly executed.

The instrumentation on the instructor's control panel automatically grades the student drivers on steering, braking, and use of turn signals. If a student forgets to turn the wheel at a corner, or turn it too little or too much, a counter on the control panel clicks off a "steering error." If someone brakes too late or too hard, or forgets to brake at all, the counter records a "braking error" for that car.

All new drivers (and even some more experienced ones!) make errors at first, until they learn the amount of response that the simulator expects. The simulator has been programmed to act just like an average automobile; if not treated like one it won't give a good grade on the performance.

After a few sessions in the simulator, you would find the driver's seat beginning to feel comfortable, the controls familiar. You would begin to perform smoothly and correctly the maneuvers called for in the film. That, of course, is the object of simulator training—to give the beginner-driver experience, or training, in the basic operations of driving. You would become so familiar with steering, signaling, shifting, braking, recognizing signs, maneuvering through intersections, and so on, that you

*Students learning to operate automobile controls
in a driver-training simulator. Road scene appears
on the screen at the front of the room.*

would be ready to perform these operations on the highway.

There's more to driving than just steering, signaling, and shifting, of course. There are city streets, traffic, pedestrians, intersections, warning signs, dogs, pot-holes, and the possibilities of emergencies of many kinds. Each new lesson in the simulator brings a reel of film that takes the student through more and more com-plicated driving situations, until the last lesson, which might have you whizzing fearlessly on and off high-speed freeways.

Of course, no one can actually learn to drive a car on a high-speed freeway by sitting in a driver-training sim-ulator and pretending to drive in a traffic scene pro-jected onto a screen. But a student who has had simulator training is better prepared for on-the-road in-struction, because he or she is already familiar with the controls and their operation and can therefore devote full attention to the road. The simulator is, above all, a *safe* place in which to learn the basic skills of driving. Mistakes here don't matter. But a mistake out on the real highway among real pedestrians, cars, trucks, and buses could place the student, the instructor, the car, and other people and vehicles in real danger.

For all its advantages, the driver-training simulator is not a true simulator because the motion picture on the screen does not respond to the actions of the "driver." That is, it doesn't stop when the driver brakes, or show movement to one side or the other as he or she steers left or right. The driver doesn't perceive the bumps, noise, acceleration, tilting, and other sensations that are experienced in a real automobile on the highway. On most simulators the instruments—gas gauge, oil-pressure gauge, temperature-warning light—can't be used to simulate emergency problems for the student to solve. Such driver-training devices are more accurately described as *trainers* rather than *simulators.*

Trainers could be built that would give the student a more complete simulation. Such a trainer would be complex and costly, but it would make the student feel as though he or she was in a real automobile on a real highway. It could be designed, for example, to move the screen view of the highway to the right or left as the student steers, and to speed up or slow down the scene as the car does. It could be designed to show what might happen if the driver ran a red light or had to swerve to avoid a dog in the street. Such a trainer would come closer to being a true simulator and would be able to provide more advanced training and thus reduce the amount of instruction required on the highway.

Simulators that can accurately reproduce the actions and sensations of real vehicles are used regularly in the field of aviation. A flight in a simulator of this kind was described in Chapter One. Such a simulator displays to the crew a simulation that is so close to the actual flight experience that the crew can scarcely tell the difference. Flight crews can be so fully trained in such simulators that only a small amount of training, if any, in a real airplane is necessary.

The first simulator was in fact invented for use in the field of aviation by Edwin C. Link in 1929. Link was a pioneer aviator who joined his passion for flight with the manufacturing know-how he learned working in his father's business, which was quite unrelated to aviation: Edwin Link's father built player pianos and pipe organs.

THREE

ED LINK INVENTS
THE "PILOT MAKER"

The first successful man-carrying, powered airplane, flown by Orville and Wilbur Wright at Kitty Hawk, North Carolina, in 1903, was such a new and startling development that neither the government, the military, nor private industry really knew what to do with it at first. Consequently, five years passed before the Wright brothers were able to sell an airplane to the United States Army.

Edwin C. Link's first successful aviation trainer was also not put to practical use until about five years after its invention. In 1934, an urgent need suddenly developed for such a trainer in aviation. The need was not the one that Link had envisioned—to give student pilots experience at airplane controls more cheaply in the first stages of their training—but rather to train pilots for the difficult task of flying airplanes through clouds, fog and the night sky by using various instruments on the airplane panel when the pilot could not see the ground or the horizon.

FROM ORGANS
TO AIRPLANES

Ed Link conceived the idea of an airplane trainer because he was a pilot, and knew from experience that such a trainer would be useful. He was able to design and build the first Link Aviation Trainer because he was also a skilled pipe organ builder.

As a boy, Link was intensely interested in all kinds of machines, especially motorcycles and airplanes. He took his first flying lesson while still in his teens, using money he had earned working in a motorcycle garage. But flying was new and very expensive in the 1920s. His first one-hour lesson cost fifty dollars. Because it took a couple of weeks of work in those days to earn fifty dollars, Link could not afford to continue his training.

He went to work in his father's factory, learning to make player pianos and pipe organs. He quickly became an expert in the mechanisms of pianos and organs, and invented many improvements and gadgets that he could see were needed.

In those days organs did not make music by means of electronic equipment and loudspeakers in use today. Instead they pumped air through pipes—one for each musical note—which caused the air to vibrate with audible musical tones. The keys and pedals the organist operated were connected to valves that directed the flow of air through the hundreds of pipes.

INVENTION OF
THE "PILOT MAKER"

Besides making music, air pressure could be used to make things move. Organ builders knew a lot about controlling airflow and moving things with air. Many years later, Link stated that without his experience in organ building, he would never have been able to build the first Pilot Maker.

The idea for the Pilot Maker was inspired by the high cost of flying. Because he couldn't afford flying lessons, Link began hanging around with "barnstormers"—wandering pilots who put on air shows and sold airplane rides from the nearest hayfield in the early days of aviation. By helping as a ground crewman, ticket salesman, and mechanic, Link earned a flying lesson now and then, and finally was allowed to take an airplane up by himself. He was so thrilled by his first solo flight that he later described it as "the first accomplishment" of his life. The organ experience, the barnstorming adventures, and his first solo flight were all important steps on the way toward his even greater accomplishment—the invention of the simulator.

In 1928, Ed Link left his father's organ factory to try his hand in the aviation business. He bought an airplane—the very first airplane sold by the new Cessna Aircraft Company. Now getting enough flying time was no problem, but he still remembered those lean years when he longed to fly but was unable to afford it. He remembered that when a friend would let him, he would taxi the friend's airplane all over the airport without flying it, just to get the feel of the airplane and its controls. He learned that the French had used this method of training fliers on the ground. They called it the "penguin system," after the flightless bird of the Antarctic.

Link began to think about building a device that could be used to give preliminary flight instruction on the ground. He designed a simulated airplane cockpit, mounted on a pivot, that would move in response to the stick and rudder, just as an airplane would. He measured the responses of actual airplanes—how far an airplane would tilt upward, for example, in response to control-stick movement. He wanted his trainer to "fly" as much like an airplane as possible.

That is how his organ-building experience paid off. He used air pumps, valves, and air bellows to make his trainer move in response to its controls. Slowly, in the basement of the organ factory, the trainer began to take shape, and in 1929 it was finished and patented. As in the case of the Wright brothers' airplane, the world was very slow to become interested. An article in a 1930 issue of the magazine *Science and Invention* described Link's invention and suggested that "Such devices would make a valuable adjunct to the multitude of miniature golf courses that now dot the country."

The suggestion was a useful one. Although amusement was not at all what Link had in mind, he took advantage of that market. He built some fifty simple models of the Pilot Maker and sold them as amusement devices for $300 to $500 each. This simplified model was equipped with a coin box like those used on hobby horses and other rides in amusement areas, and with a device for grading the "pilot's" skill.

But Link strongly believed that his invention was no mere toy or amusement device, but a device that could really train pilots. By using it in his own flying school and demonstrating its value whenever and to whomever he could, Link finally began to sell a few trainers to the aviation industry.

But these were the years of the Great Depression, and money for everything was tight. Link's tiny company struggled to stay afloat. The first simple Pilot Makers for the aviation industry sold for only about $450, the more elaborate ones with flight instruments, $1,500. Although the U.S. military air services began to see the value of the Pilot Maker for training pilots, they lacked the money to buy them.

The first Pilot Maker for the aviation industry was bought by the Pioneer Instrument Company, which used it to demonstrate and experiment with the trio of instruments that are needed to fly an airplane when ground and horizon are not visible: the magnetic compass, the airspeed indicator, and the key instrument, the turn-and-bank indicator, which enables the pilot to control the turning of the plane. With this sale, the Pilot Maker moved closer to the use in which it would ultimately succeed: training pilots to fly "on instruments."

In 1934 a catastrophe occurred that gave a boost to Link's company. In February of that year the U.S. Army Air Corps was ordered to fly the airmail in the United States. Army pilots then had little experience in flying at night or in bad weather "on instruments" and had only old, inadequate airplanes. Five pilots were killed in the first few days of flying the mail.

LINK TO
THE RESCUE

The Army quickly began to search for solutions to its problem, and arranged for Link to come to Newark Airport in New Jersey to demonstrate his machine. This visit began with an unexpected and dramatic event. When the Army group reached the airport, the weather was too bad, they thought, for Link to arrive by air. As they turned to leave, they heard his plane above in the overcast. He landed safely. Link succeeded in convincing the Army that instrument flight was practical and could be taught by his trainer.

*Ed Link (far right) with other aviation pioneers,
including Charles A. Lindbergh (far left)*

Factory assembly line for early Link Trainers

Despite this demonstration and the Army's great need for Link's trainer, the money could not be found for purchase. But with the help of knowledgeable congressmen, an emergency appropriation was passed by the Congress, and within two months six Pilot Makers were ordered.

This was the breakthrough Link needed. Within a few years, Link trainers were also flowing from his factory to air forces in Europe. The Japanese military began to order trainers for its pilot-training program. Ironically, a few years later pilots trained in the new Pilot Maker in Europe, America, and Japan would be facing each other in combat in World War II.

Ed Link's invention, originally aimed at teaching students the basics of how to fly an airplane, had suddenly been accepted for a much more difficult task—teaching pilots to fly an airplane on instruments in bad weather.

FOUR

AIRPLANE SIMULATORS

In the early days of aviation, pilots used to brag about "flying by the seat of their pants" when they couldn't see the ground in bad weather. Is it really possible to fly without seeing the ground? What is the origin of the expression "flying by the seat of one's pants?"

The answer to the first question is that without special instruments in the airplane, and the skill to use them, a pilot is almost helpless when the ground or the horizon cannot be seen, and is almost certain to lose control and crash.

The problem is that we humans do not have the ability to tell which way is "up" when we can't see the ground. The *Instrument-Flying Handbook,* published by the Federal Aviation Administration, says "Your body is not designed for flight. You are equipped to operate as a ground animal . . . adapted to movement on the ground through sensory systems that you react to through habit."

If you have no view of the horizon, you have no way of knowing whether or not your wings are level. Because the forces on your body in flight are different from those on the ground, you can't tell whether the airplane is flying "straight and level" or turning.

THE NEED
FOR INSTRUMENTS

If you sit on a chair (on the ground) and lean to one side, the force of gravity, which pulls you toward the earth, tends to tip you out of the chair, and your balance system gives you the feeling that you are leaning. In an airplane, however, the lift force that supports the airplane (and you in your seat) is not aimed at the center of the earth, but remains perpendicular to the wings as the airplane banks in a turn (Figure 1). The pilot thus does not have the sensation of leaning to one side when

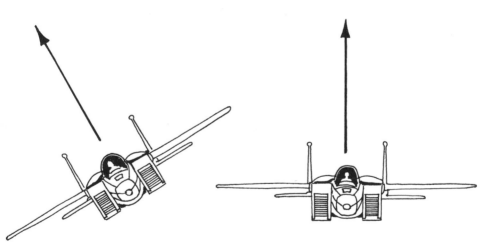

Figure 1. Occupants of an aircraft can sense no difference between level and banked (turning) flight because the lift force supporting the airplane is always perpendicular to the wing.

the wings are not level. Because the forces felt on "the seat of the pants" are the same whether the airplane is flying straight and level or in a diving turn, the pilot cannot, with his or her own senses, keep the airplane in level flight. The compass will eventually show that the airplane is turning, but the compass is not sufficiently sensitive to tell the pilot quickly enough that the airplane is turning, and in which direction. In rough air, the compass may spin crazily at times. By the time the compass has shown that the airplane is turning, and the altimeter and airspeed indicator have shown that it is descending, the pilot may be in a dangerous spiral dive, perhaps unable to figure out which way to turn to return to level flight. If the pilot cannot stop this spiral quickly, or if he turns the wrong way, the airplane may turn upside down or stress its wings to the breaking point and end up crashing.

The instrument that can tell the pilot whether the airplane is turning is actually one of the simplest on the control panel. The heart of the instrument is a small, heavy, spinning wheel, like those in toy gyroscopes. When the airplane turns, the spinning gyroscope wheel resists being turned, and causes a needle deflection on the face of the instrument. In flight, if this needle is centered (no deflection) the pilot knows that the airplane is not turning. By banking the airplane to reach a certain needle deflection, the pilot can make a shallow or steep turn, as needed.

This simple "turn-and-bank" indicator, as it is called, made the difference between life and death when a pilot was suddenly caught in bad weather. With this instrument, an altimeter, an airspeed indicator, and some training in their use, a pilot could keep the airplane right side up, on a straight course, at the proper speed, and maneuver it correctly toward its destination while "flying blind" through clouds.

Though not in regular use in those days, the turn-and-bank indicator was on the simple instrument panel of the *Spirit of St. Louis* in which Charles Lindbergh made his historic nonstop flight from New York to Paris in 1927. Without it, he could not have safely flown through the many miles of bad weather that he encountered over the Atlantic Ocean.

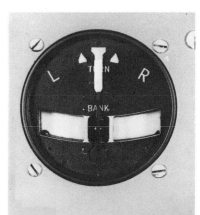

The turn-and-bank indicator that made early instrument flight possible. The white pointer shows when the plane is turning right or left. The black ball moves right or left in the curved tube to show the plane is skidding in its turn.

Below: Instrument panel of "The Spirit of St. Louis." Turn-and-bank indicator is in bottom row (center).

FLYING
BY INSTRUMENTS

But it is not enough to be able to just maneuver the airplane and keep it right side up. The pilot must be able to follow a course through the sky, find the airport, and descend safely to the runway. Early radio aids provided an instrument needle that pointed toward low-frequency "radio beacons" or an aural signal that told the pilot, through earphones, when the flight was on the airway (the designated route along which an airplane flies). These systems were crude and unreliable, and were made almost useless by "static" near thunderstorms. They have been replaced by high-frequency radio and other modern aids. These allow the pilot to follow an exact path in the sky from takeoff to landing, whatever the visibility and weather conditions, for the same reason that "FM" (high frequency) radios work well in any weather, whereas "AM" (low frequency) radios sometimes have heavy static.

The pilot must become highly skilled in the use of all this equipment, and that requires training and practice. Driving a car is easy by comparison. There are only two things to watch and control in a car: speed and direction. In an airplane, the pilot must control speed, direction, altitude, vertical motion (climbing or descending), and banking. To control all of these motions "on instruments," the pilot must learn to move his or her attention from one flight instrument to another rapidly, making corrections to course, altitude, speed, and bank angle in quick succession. This is a demanding task that requires much practice to perform correctly, especially in rough air or bad weather.

The pilot must simultaneously operate the radio aids to follow the desired route, monitor the engine instruments and controls, and plan and execute the descent to the unseen runway for a landing.

SIMULATORS
TO THE RESCUE

When Army Air Corps pilots were ordered to fly the mail, they lacked the needed complex skills and equipment. Training Army pilots in these skills was the task of Link's early Pilot Maker.

As airplanes grew more complex over the years—greater size, more engines, radar, pressurization, greater speed, higher altitudes—the number of gauges and controls in the cockpit and the duties of the pilot all increased enormously. If pilots did not watch their engine instruments carefully enough, there were more chances of engine failures. Instruments such as fuel-quantity indicators and engine-temperature gauges were added to simulators to train the pilot to monitor this vital information. If the pilot failed to notice that fuel was running low or the engine was too hot, the simulator would make the "engine" run rough and eventually "quit." As military airplanes acquired more and more fighting equipment—guns, bombs, rockets, radar, fire-control systems—all of which had to be operated by the pilot or another crew member, these items were added to simulators for these aircraft.

SIMULATORS FOR
OTHER CREW FUNCTIONS

The need for training other members of military air crews was soon recognized, and new types of trainers and simulators were built to teach needed skills to gun-

*The cockpit of a modern aircraft simulator
exactly duplicates the cockpit of the airplane
itself, with all controls functional.*

ners, radar operators, navigators, and bombardiers. The Celestial Navigation Trainer (CNT), developed in 1941, was one of the most remarkable of the new simulators. It had crew stations for pilot, bombardier, and navigator, and a dome overhead on which was projected nearly 400 stars, much like a planetarium. The stars moved across the sky as the airplane moved on its simulated mission, so that sighting the stars with a navigator's sextant at any point in the flight would tell the navigator the airplane's position on the map at that time. A full mission could be flown in this simulator, with the navigator, pilot, and bombardier all performing the tasks required to fly and navigate the bomber to the target and return.

Over the years, simulators grew rapidly in size and complexity, and in contrast to the original Pilot Maker, which cost a few hundred dollars, present-day large airplane simulators can cost many millions of dollars.

After World War II, simulators increasingly came to be operated by computers instead of air bellows, levers, and motors. Simulators for transport airplanes became near-perfect duplicates of actual airplane cockpits, with full, working instrumentation and controls. A computer-generated moving view of the ground through the windshield was added, to give the pilot the illusion of flying the airplane all the way down to the runway. At "touchdown," the simulator even provided a squeak and a jolt when the tires touched the pavement.

Airplane simulators are now used in almost all phases of pilot training. If you take flying lessons, you are likely to be offered the chance to use simpler simulators, such as the Link General Aviation Trainer (GAT), in your primary flight training and basic instrument training. The Link GAT is somewhat like the origi-

General Aviation Trainer (GAT) simulates
the cockpit of light aircraft. Instructor (outside) also plays role of air-traffic controller.

nal Link machine, modified to resemble the cockpit of a modern light airplane. Simulator training helps a new student to learn the basics about airplane controls and procedures under relaxed conditions before moving to the more stressful training conditions of real flight.

The more complex full-airplane simulators are used extensively by airlines and the military for advanced training in heavy multiengine aircraft. So exact is the simulation of particular aircraft that simulators are used regularly to qualify pilots to fly different types and models of aircraft. An airline pilot may take all of his training and qualification tests for an airplane he hasn't flown before in a simulator. The pilot may not actually fly the real airplane until leaving the runway for the first time with a full load of passengers in the cabin.

FIVE

HOW SIMULATORS WORK

The airplane simulator is a complicated machine, but what it is *supposed* to do can be simply stated: its job is to pretend that it is an airplane. The airplane simulator generally consists of: (1) a pilot's station (or stations); (2) controls and switches for the pilot to operate; (3) mechanisms or computers to do the "pretending"; and (4) instrument dials for the pilot to read. The mechanisms or computers use the movement of the controls and switches to indicate on the dials and gauges what these control movements would do if performed on an actual airplane.

Figure 2 schematically shows the pilot at the controls of a real airplane. When the pilot moves a control, the airplane does something—speeds up, slows down, climbs, descends, banks, or whatever—and this action is interpreted back to the pilot as an indication on one or more of the panel instruments. From this information, the pilot learns what the airplane is doing in response to the control movement made, and can make the next control movement to keep the airplane doing what he or she wants it to do.

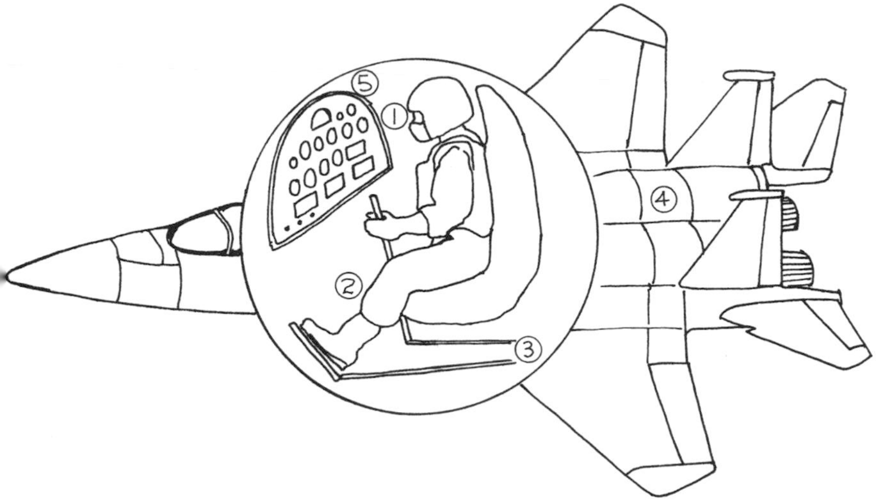

Figure 2. Flow of actions and information in a real airplane: (1) pilot reads instruments; (2) pilot moves controls; (3) controls move wing flaps, engine throttle, etc.; (4) airplane responds with changes in attitude and speed; (5) new information on airplane motion is measured by instruments on panel.

MACHINES THAT PRETEND

Figure 3 shows that the same thing happens in a simulator, except that the controls and instruments are not connected to a real airplane, but to a box of mechanisms or computers that can *pretend* it is an airplane. The box takes the pilot's control movement, calculates what the airplane would do, and returns that information to the pilot on the panel instruments. The pilot can learn, or practice, flying an airplane by "flying" this machine that can *pretend* it is an airplane.

As we learned earlier, early simulators were built of electrical circuits, motors, relays, levers, push-rods, and

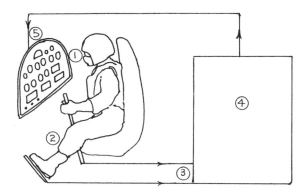

Figure 3. The flow of actions and information in an aircraft simulator: (1) pilot reads instruments; (2) pilot moves controls; (3) control motion goes to computer; (4) computer calculates changes (attitude, speed, etc.) control motions would produce on real airplane; (5) new information on calculated motions of "airplane" are sent to panel instruments.

air bellows. As the airplanes to be simulated became more and more complicated, it became obvious that simulators built this way would be far too large, slow, and complicated. Fortunately, computer technology came along in time to make a whole new kind of simulator possible, one in which nearly all actions are performed by high-speed computers. The familiarity that most of us have acquired with computers at school, at home, or at work makes it easier to understand how the computer-driven simulator works.

FLYING
AN AIRPLANE

To learn how the simulator does its job, let's examine first what happens when the pilot of a real airplane moves a control—to increase the power output of the engine, for example. When the pilot pushes the throttle forward, the real engine responds by putting out increased power, and the airplane speeds up and will begin to climb. To adjust the climb, the pilot may pull back on the stick or control wheel at the same time (or push forward to maintain the same flight level at an increased speed).

The instruments on the panel tell the pilot what the airplane is doing: the altimeter will show increasing altitude, the airspeed meter will show any change in speed, engine instruments will show any change in engine temperature.

FLYING
A SIMULATOR

If the same maneuver is performed in a simulator, the movement of the throttle does not tell an engine to increase power, but instead gives a computer a new throttle setting from which it can calculate a new value of engine thrust. This value is then placed in the "data pool" in the computer's memory, where it is immediately picked up by another computer and used, along with the new control wheel position, to calculate a new value of airplane speed and rate of climb. That information is sent to the airspeed indicator and the altimeter on the panel to show the pilot the result of the control movement, and to the data pool.

Another computer dips into the data pool, takes the increased engine power and uses it to calculate the fuel being used. The fuel remaining in the tank is also calculated and placed on the fuel-quantity gauge on the panel. This data goes back to the data pool too, to be picked up by yet another computer and used in the calculation of a new airplane weight, which is in turn returned to the data pool to be used in a new calculation of airspeed and climb rate. That computer, of course, is also using the changing altitude (changing air density) to recalculate airspeed and altitude, over and over again. The engine-power computer also uses the changing air density to recalculate engine power (as the "airplane" climbs), which is then used to recalculate airspeed, and so on. Because every change in what the "airplane" does changes nearly everything else, the computers must rapidly and continuously recalculate all of these things, over and over again.

For another example, assume that the pilot operates the handle that puts down the airplane's "landing gear" as he or she approaches the "runway" in the simulator. The computer has in its memory the increased drag that the landing gear will produce. It immediately calculates the decreasing speed of the airplane, as well as the slight diving tendency and other effects that the increased landing-gear drag will produce, and puts this information on all the appropriate instruments on the panel. The pilot sees these results and makes corrections, such as adding power and pulling the nose up with an elevator deflection. The computer takes these pilot actions and recalculates the speed and flight altitude of the "airplane," and the process continues as the pilot works the controls to keep the "airplane" on the descent path it needs to reach the airport runway.

The pilot of the simulator is really "flying" a computer that acts just like an airplane. The computer calculates all the things that the airplane would do with the control movements put in by the pilot, and shows the pilot the results on the instruments and gauges.

How does the computer "know" just what the air-plane would do with a certain control input? The characteristics of the airplane are programmed in advance into the computer. The engineers designing the simulator must know how the airplane flies, in other words, so that they can "teach" the simulator, through its computer software, to mimic the airplane. For this reason, a simulator for a particular airplane can be built and "flown" only after the airplane itself has been designed and its flight characteristics measured or calculated.

Sometimes pilots have complained that a new simulator did not "fly" like the real airplane. When the simulator engineers and the airplane engineers got together and tracked down the problem, they found that the computer had not been correctly programmed, perhaps because the characteristics of the airplane had not been correctly predicted. When the error was corrected in the computer software, pilots usually found that the simulator did indeed "fly" just like the real airplane.

The computer at the heart of the simulator is, of course, very complex. It is actually a bank of as many as 50 to 125 or more separate modules, each of which for all practical purposes is a separate computer, more or less like the small computer that you may have operated in school or at home.

A master control is in charge of the whole operation. Each module signals the master when it has finished its calculations, and the master then tells the next module to perform its task. Each module takes only a split second to perform its calculations, and the entire system sweeps through all its computations many times each second. Because the process is repeated so rapidly, the instrument readings that the pilot sees change gradually and smoothly, just as they would in a real airplane.

FULL-MISSION SIMULATORS

The modern airline simulator is designed not only to maneuver like an airplane but also to simulate a full mission, including the two most important parts, the takeoff and the landing. In takeoff, the pilot must accelerate straight down the runway, rotate the airplane into the air, retract the landing gear, follow the departure pattern given by Air Traffic Control to the assigned airway, and cope with any emergencies—such as failure of an engine—in the process. In the landing approach, the pilot must follow the instruments until the ground is visible, then look out the windshield and land the airplane on the runway, and apply thrust reversers and brakes to slow down before the airplane runs off the end of the runway. Because these are important parts of a flight, full-mission simulators are built to give the crew a simulated view of the ground through the windshield.

Some early simulators provided windshield views by projecting on a screen ahead of the windshield actual motion pictures of the runway taken from an approaching aircraft. Others used television views provided by a television camera moving over a scale model of the ground (and airport runway) in another room. The camera in the model scene was moved by a computer to give a view correct for the airplane's position on the descent or climb-out path. These methods of simulating a view of the ground were cumbersome and limited in accuracy, and have been all but abandoned.

Newer simulators use computer-generated views of the airport and vicinity that move very accurately as the airplane moves. The image shown has been designed to correspond to a particular airport, in color for daytime scenes, or as a pattern of lights on bridges, streets, and tall buildings for nighttime scenes. Airport runways and taxiways are accurately depicted by rows of appropriately colored lights—white for runways, blue for taxiways, and so on. The simulation, particularly of the nighttime scene, is so realistic that the simulator crew has a strong illusion that they are actually descending in an airplane toward a real airport and a real runway.

NOISES, JOLTS AND OTHER SENSATIONS

Other sensations are also provided, such as sound and acceleration, to further accentuate the illusion of flying. The crew can hear the sound of the landing gear operating. The computer generates a "tire squeak" when the airplane "touches down," and directs the hydraulic pistons supporting the whole pilot compartment to deliver a sudden jolt that can be either slight or strong, depending on how skillfully the pilot has set the plane down.

The whole cockpit can be made to bounce around when the instructor directs the computer to pretend that the airplane is flying in rough air. During the takeoff run of a real airplane, the crew is pressed back into their seats by the rapid increase in speed, just as you are when you are in an accelerating automobile. In the simulator, the whole pilot compartment, up on its lanky stiltlike legs, is tilted back by hydraulic mechanisms to cause the crew's body weight to press them into the backs of their seats. When the thrust reversers and brakes are applied after landing, the compartment is tilted forward to make the crew feel that they are being pulled forward in response to deceleration. The crew cannot see this tilting motion, because the whole cockpit, and everything that they see, including the windshield view, tilts with them.

SIMULATOR MISSIONS

The missions or flight profiles that pilots fly in their training sessions, like the flight described in Chapter One, are out of the ordinary. The simulator instructor at the desk in the back area of the "cockpit" sees to that. He can be mischievous, if he likes, giving the crew one emergency after another, turning on lightning and rough air, knocking out radio aids, producing instrument failures, setting engine fires—all to test and improve the skills of the crew in handling emergencies that might happen in flight.

Little experience in handling serious emergencies could be safely given to air crews in real airplanes. Prior to the use of simulators, in fact, many aircraft and crews were lost due to accidents that took place while practicing even modest emergencies. In simulators, even the most desperate emergency or dangerous maneuver can be practiced, over and over again if necessary, in complete safety. Events that result in an accident can be simulated and "flown" again and again to find out what caused the accident, and to learn whether it might have been avoided.

One fatal crash occurred when one engine dropped off a large passenger airliner right after takeoff. Could that accident have been prevented? The simulator tests said yes, if the pilots had been able instantly to do exactly the right things to retain control of the aircraft. The new knowledge from such simulator tests is passed on to pilots to help prevent other, similar crashes.

Simulators have been used to investigate what happens in "wind-shear" situations—those sudden bursts of downdrafts or irregular winds at low altitude that can suddenly reduce the airspeed of an airplane and may, in the extreme case, cause it to lose lift and crash. New operating procedures have been devised in such simulations to help pilots to fly out of such emergencies and avoid a crash.

When Ed Link invented the simulator, he could not have imagined how important it would eventually become to aviation. Nor could he have guessed that simulators would one day be built to train people to perform dozens of other complex tasks in transportation and industry.

MILITARY COMBAT SIMULATORS: DOGFIGHT IN A BOX

"Squadron Commander, this is Speed Bird Two. I've got a computer lock on the enemy aircraft at flight level four two zero, bearing zero one five, range twenty-two miles, closing speed six hundred miles per hour, preparing to fire missile, over."

Such a radio message suggests that this airplane is on a mission far different from flying passengers or mail or freight from one point to another. Alone in the airplane, hurtling through the night sky at nearly the speed of sound, searching with radar for an unseen aircraft, the pilot must identify the aircraft as an enemy; plan a course to intercept it; choose, aim, and fire a weapon to shoot it down. All the while, the pilot must also be alert to the possibility that someone else is trying to shoot *him* down.

With a high-speed fighter airplane to fly, weapons systems to operate, radars and computers to control, the pilot of a military interceptor has a great deal to do—even more than you might realize.

There are more than a dozen buttons and switches that must be operated, but the pilot's hands and feet are already busy. Feet operate the rudder pedals, the right hand grasps a control "stick" that operates the airplane's elevators and ailerons, the left hand operates the engine throttle. The dozen buttons are located in the only place available—on the control handles where fingers can activate them.

The buttons control many different functions. Many, in fact, do more than one thing; these are called multifunction switches. For example, one of the buttons on the pilot's control stick operates the combat radar. Pushing the button once changes the range of how far ahead the radar will search for enemy aircraft. Pushing it again steps the radar to a different range, and so on. By sliding the same switch up or down, the pilot can "tilt" the radar to look "up" or "down" ahead of the aircraft. A final push of the same button places a gun sight on the windshield for aiming and firing a weapon. That's a lot of important things for one switch to do, and a lot for the pilot to learn.

As if that's not enough, that same switch has yet another function. If the aircraft is engaged in aerial refueling and the refueling door is open, then that same button automatically becomes an emergency disconnect switch to uncouple the fighter from the tanker aircraft.

There are four more buttons on the control stick in the pilot's right hand alone. The left hand, which grips the throttle quadrant, has another seven buttons to operate with the fingers of that hand. These buttons control items such as aircraft flight control trim, nose gear steering on the ground, and the radio microphone. One button controls secret surveillance computers which can help the pilot to identify instantly whether an aircraft on the radarscope is an enemy. If the computer detects an enemy plane, the pilot can press another button to ask the computer exactly what type of aircraft it is. Still more buttons select the types of missiles or bombs or guns to be fired. A final button, at the fingertip, actually fires the weapons. More than a dozen functions may be controlled in each hand, all in addition to the normal workload of flying the aircraft.

How can a military fighter pilot be trained to handle all this complex equipment—radar, computers, guns, rockets, bombs—while flying the aircraft, safely and economically? The answer, of course, is in the simulator—or, as pilots often say, in "the box."

A fighter simulator sometimes consists of two separate cockpits, linked together by computers and connected to an instructor's console. These separate cockpits—often referred to as "black boxes" by aviators—allow two fighter pilots to practice many different air-to-air combat missions. For example, they can "fly" missions against each other, or they can "fly formation" together as a team against a common "enemy" aircraft. All this can be done "in the box," without leaving the ground, without danger, without launching real weapons or burning any fuel.

Both pilots have computer-generated images on their screens that look just like the terrain below and the sky above. These images move to give the view the pilot would have in an airplane when doing any of the maneuvers needed in combat flying—a roll, a loop, a dive or a steep climb. If the fighter draws close to the target aircraft, each pilot has a visual display of the "adver-

Military tactical ("dogfight") simulator consists of two separate cockpits linked by computers and instructor's consoles. Each pilot sees a computer-generated image of his adversary through his windshield.

sary" on the windshield—a computer image of the aircraft flown by the pilot in the other simulator.

To begin the mission, the simulator instructor may start the two aircraft far away from each other. The student then learns to control those buttons on the control sticks to conduct a radar search for the enemy. At first, the other plane will show up as merely a blip on the pilot's radar screen. Using still more buttons, the pilot learns to track and then identify the blip. If the target aircraft gets close—within sight of the pursuing aircraft—the simulator's computer provides an image in the pilot's view that looks like an actual aircraft. This effect is usually done by using a model of the enemy aircraft, complete with movable flight controls, enemy paint colors and insignia. A television camera in another room films the exact movements of the model as it is "flown" by the "enemy" simulator pilot, to provide this image.

Newer simulators use "computer generated" images of the target airplanes. In either case, if the simulator pilots are teamed up to fly against an "enemy" aircraft, the "enemy" or "target" aircraft being pursued is flown by the instructor at his console. This target aircraft is then brought by television to the fighter pilots' view in both cockpits. The details may be so realistic that the pilot can see the flight controls on the surface of the wings or tail move. The pilot can also watch for the target aircraft to suddenly switch on the afterburner in an attempt to pull up and away fast, or operate the speedbrake panels, in an effort to dive abruptly and get away.

In the heat of a chase, the attacker or the quarry use the enormous power, speed, and quick maneuverability of the fighter aircraft to make sudden accelerations or

*Computer simulation of target
aircraft image as seen by pilot*

maneuvers. The pilots feel these forces of acceleration
on their bodies. Some high-speed maneuvers can exert
forces on the body that would make the person feel as
though he or she weighed 400, 600, even 1,000
pounds. These forces are called G-forces and are measured as multiples of gravity. During an 8-G maneuver,
for example, a 170-pound man will feel as though he
weighs 8 times real body weight, or 1,360 pounds. Simulators can't duplicate these G forces because they are
all but motionless on the ground. But the computer can
show the pilot the effect his acceleration might have on
his vision. If the acceleration moves toward the point of

pilot blackout (unconsciousness), as measured by the G-meter, the simulator further warns the pilot of that condition by actually dimming the lights in the cockpit.

Aerial dogfights are the most demanding type of flying, both on pilots and aircraft. Such maneuvers require a fighter pilot to use all the tricks available and all his senses. It's important that the simulator duplicate all the details found in a real airplane, such as changing engine sounds, the motions and vibrations resulting from the flow of air over the aircraft, and others. All such sounds provide clues about what the airplane is doing while the student is engaged in a mission against an enemy aircraft. Even sun glints can be generated to give instant and realistic clues as to the enemy aircraft's evasive maneuvers.

The training session may end when the student chooses a weapon with his buttons—missile or gun—and fires it against the attacker. That is, of course, unless the enemy, the pilot in the other simulator, blasts him first! The simulator actually responds to the firing of the gun or to the launch of a missile, giving the pilot the sounds, sights, and movements he would see and feel in a real airplane.

The simulator's computers record weapon firings, then compute and record hits or misses. The complete combat engagement can be played back, in whole or in part, for the pilots and their instructors to discuss.

The combat simulator thus provides a means for training fighter pilots far removed from the risks of actual combat. Not only do the pilots learn to fly their complex high-speed jets, they also learn to use the double handfuls of switches and buttons that will eventually be critical to their survival in real combat.

HELICOPTER
GUNSHIPS THAT
ACTUALLY GO BANG!

Military helicopter gunships regularly fly missions that are quite different from those of other military aircraft. They often fly close to the ground, sometimes at treetop level, in daylight or dark or foul weather, searching out low-flying aircraft or ground targets. They are armed with rockets, grenades, and guns. In combat action they may face enemy groundfire and must be able to maneuver quickly to survive. The crew, consisting of pilot and copilot-gunner, must not only be skilled at flying the helicopter. They must also be accomplished gunners, thoroughly trained in the use of all their weapons.

To train for this kind of dangerous combat flying in real helicopters would be risky and costly. Yet it is essential that helicopter gunship crews learn to use their specialized equipment under conditions as close as possible to the combat situation.

For training gunship crews, a simulator is used that can pretend it is a helicopter with all its armaments and unusual maneuvering abilities. Computers simulate not only the armaments and weapons available to the crew, but also create the battle scenes and conditions that such a gunship would encounter in real fighting.

Helicopter gunship simulators consist of two stations. One duplicates the pilot's cockpit, the other the copilot-gunner's position. A computer can link the two together as though they were in one aircraft on a single mission. Or the separate stations can be operated independently to give specific training to pilot or gunner alone.

Cockpit of the helicopter simulator has
computer-generated views out the window.

A detailed model of the terrain—complete with roads, bridges, trees, towns, and street lights—is photographed by a miniature video camera which maneuvers near the model, corresponding to the simulated flight path of the aircraft. Some newer simulators show the crew computer-generated views of the terrain and targets. The crew members may be in full battle dress and equipped with helmet gun sights for aiming their battery of weapons against targets that pass by below. The video through their front and side windows may also project tracer flashes from groundfire below. An authentic sound-simulation system makes this simulator a realistically noisy place to be when all those weapons are firing.

ANTISUBMARINE WARFARE SIMULATORS

Submarines have long been used by navies all over the world. They are so widely used because they are particularly difficult to detect. They dive deep, are engineered to run very quietly, and can lie silent for long periods of time to avoid detection.

Modern submarines carry several kinds of lethal weapons aboard for attacking other vessels as well as cities and military targets on land. It is important for a nation's navy and air services to be able to detect, track, and if necessary, destroy an enemy submarine in a wartime situation. The first task of antisubmarine warfare (ASW) forces is to find the submarine. The complicated instruments and sonar equipment this task requires are used not only on naval ships, but aircraft and helicopters as well. This complex detection gear is quite similar in operation and purpose, whether on ship or in the air.

Although water transmits sound far better than air does, the problem of searching for the sounds of a submarine under vast oceans is complicated by several things. First, water often provides an excellent shield to confuse searchers. Sound paths change and bend underwater as a result of water depth, water temperature at different depths, saltiness, and the distance and direction the sound waves must travel. Even the landscape of the ocean's floor may alter the sound signal. All these variables may mask, distort, and bend the sound of the submarine's engines and propellers, which makes it difficult to find and identify the enemy submarine.

ASW personnel, whether aboard ships, planes, helicopters, or other submarines, must learn to listen to and interpret all the various sounds. They do this with sonar, a system for receiving and analyzing sound. (Sonar stands for SOund NAvigation Ranging.) After identifying an enemy submarine, they must learn how to track it and finally destroy it, without getting shot at first. Simulators are used to train technical crews in this difficult job of chasing submarines around the ocean.

These simulators have some unusual phenomena to simulate: underwater noises and sounds of the ocean, and the sound of specific submarines traveling at various depths, speeds, and power settings. Once engineers have modeled these sounds and all the details of their transmission through water in the computer program, the rest of the simulation task is similar to that for other simulators already discussed.

The crew stations aboard ASW simulators are made to look exactly like the operator stations aboard aircraft,

The operators' stations of a simulator for a shipboard Antisubmarine Warfare (ASW) system

helicopters, ships, or other submarines. Since motion and outside visual references are unimportant, these simulators remain stationary and deal mainly with the sounds and echoes of deep underwater activity.

If a submarine is operating at low speed or is lying silent near the bottom, detection is particularly difficult. The trainee can switch from passive (listening) sonar to active sonar, which sends out a series of sharp sounds (called "pings") and listens for reflections, like a kind of underwater radar. Depending on whether the simulator represents a helicopter, ship, or airplane, the student will also learn to drop or "dip" remote listening buoys, or to trail metal antennas into the water to detect an enemy submarine.

Once the enemy sub is detected, the trainees then track it and close in for the attack. If successful in tracking a hostile submarine, the trainee can deploy a variety of weapons—depth charges, rockets, air-to-surface missiles, and homing torpedoes—to blow up the sub. As in other weapon simulators, the ASW simulators can calculate and record successful hits or misses. Both student and instructor know when a few more hours in the ASW simulator are needed to become more proficient at hunting submarines.

SEVEN

SPACEFLIGHT SIMULATORS: FIFTY MOON LANDINGS A DAY

In one of the first trainer-simulators used in the U.S. manned space program, the astronaut trainee lay on his back, strapped into a contoured "couch" that was designed to support his body against the crushing deceleration forces of reentry from orbit. His right hand grasped a control handle that could be moved forward or back, left or right.

"Ready?" called a voice.

The astronaut stared up at the two targets he was supposed to keep lined up, and tightened his grip on the control handle.

"Ready!"

A roar erupted beneath him, and his couch tilted and began to turn. Being a skilled airplane pilot, he moved the control instinctively in the right direction, but first too much, then too little, then the right amount. The simulator slowly swung back to the proper position. Suddenly the roar died away, but another began immediately, with the couch swinging in the opposite direction. The noise and the movement of the couch simulated the action of the retro-rockets that were to be fired on the orbiting Mercury capsule to slow the capsule below orbital speed so that it would reenter the earth's atmosphere. The turning forces of the rockets were simulated on this trainer by harmless jets of high-pressure air, but their effect was the same.

The second rocket died away as the third took over. The astronaut's reactions were quicker now, and his busy hand on the control kept the capsule pointed ahead fairly well. Suddenly, silence. The last rocket had burned out.

Because there had to be three rocket motors tightly packaged at the center of the Mercury spacecraft heat shield, none of them could be aligned with the center of gravity of the capsule. The thrust from each of the three rocket motors would tend to make the capsule twirl in a different direction. The hand controller would operate other very small liquid rocket motors out on the rim of the spacecraft to control its attitude.

This early simulation device was built to train the Mercury astronauts to keep their capsule pointed in the right direction while the rockets were firing, and later to keep its heat shield pointed in the direction of motion during reentry into the earth's atmosphere. If the capsule tumbled during rocket firing, the desired speed reduction and course for reentry would not be achieved. If the capsule was allowed to tumble during reentry, it would be destroyed if the fiery shock wave impinged on the metal shell instead of standing out ahead of the heat shield as the capsule plunged into the atmosphere.

The first trainers and simulators for the U.S. space program were, like this one, fairly simple devices built for a single purpose. Dozens more trainers and simulators followed, some of which were the most complicated simulators ever built up to that time. The first astronauts were all experienced test pilots, accustomed to making quick decisions while operating complex aircraft. However, spacecraft and spaceflight were new and different, and there were new equipment and skills to be learned. Space was not the place for astronauts to learn to fly an unfamiliar spacecraft.

Mock-ups of spacecraft control panels were built as part-task trainers. Most of these contained some "dummy," or nonoperating, switches and dials, along with many real switches that actually controlled something. After they had become familiar with all the controls and had learned all the tasks expected of them, the astronauts moved to full-mission simulators that accurately simulated nearly everything in the spacecraft. These simulators, which looked and performed just like the real thing, could be connected to the launch control center and mission control center so that controllers and space crews could practice full missions together. Like other simulators that have been described earlier, the spacecraft simulator was an exact replica of the real spacecraft and could, with the aid of its computer system, pretend that it was a real spacecraft performing a space mission.

One sensation of spaceflight that could not be simulated in the full-mission simulation was weightlessness. No machine can be built on earth that turns off gravity. But reduced gravity and even full "weightlessness" can be simulated fairly well under limited conditions. This was done with an overhead harness that supported four-fifths of the astronaut trainee's weight, leaving him with weight force on his feet equal to the force he will feel when walking on the moon. Such a simulation,

NASA engineer tries walking on a simulated lunar terrain using the lunar gravity simulator. The overhead harness lets him touch the ground with a force of only one-sixth his weight.

though crude, helped moon-bound astronauts to get used to walking and working in space suits with bulky life-support packs in the reduced gravity of the moon.

Space crews experience full "relative weightlessness" in orbital spaceflight. In orbit, both spacecraft and crew are completely under control of earth's gravity, to be sure, but they are "falling together" around the earth. Their speed keeps them out in an orbit that does fall into the surface of the earth. Because they are "falling together," there is no force between spacecraft and crew; hence, the crew is in a condition of "relative weightlessness" with respect to their spacecraft. Astronauts, tools, papers, food, dust—everything—floats around in the spacecraft in orbit as though there is no gravity.

Relative weightlessness can be exactly simulated in airplane flight at high altitude, if the airplane is flown on a path that allows airplane and occupants to "fall together" for a short time. The pilot pulls the airplane up to a high climb angle, and then pushes the nose downward until there is no lift on the airplane's wings.

How can the pilot tell when there is no lift on the airplane's wings? A small rubber ball can be suspended on a thread in front of the pilot's face for this purpose. When the thread goes limp and the ball floats in the air, the pilot knows that the ball, the airplane, and everyone in it are falling together and weightless relative to each other. Astronauts have used such flights to become familiar with the sensations and problems of moving around in relative weightlessness. They have performed a variety of duties, including climbing in and out of mock-up spacecraft hatches inside the airplane, to simulate going outside a spacecraft in pressure suits for a space "walk" in orbit.

The airplane can, of course, follow a zero-lift path only briefly. With its nose moving steadily downward to maintain zero lift on its wings, the airplane is soon pointed steeply toward the ground, and must stop falling and start flying again. The pilot first sounds a warning horn to tell the crew that gravity is about to return, then pulls the airplane back up into level flight. With the airplane supported by lift on its wings once more the occupants feel full gravity and can walk around inside the cabin as before.

Relative weightlessness can also be simulated in a tank of water, where the astronaut, in full pressure suit, is properly weighted so that he neither sinks to the bottom nor floats on top. Although moving around in water is somewhat different from moving in air, such a simulation of weightlessness can be useful. Astronauts in full pressure suits can experience the problems of using tools, entering and leaving a spacecraft mock-up, and even assembling small structures in space.

MOON-MISSION
SIMULATORS

In the Apollo program it was necessary to train crews for several very complex operations during the moon mission. For example, the Lunar Landing Module, on returning from the surface of the moon, had to link up, or rendezvous, with the Command Module in lunar orbit. These two vehicles had to be brought together with scarcely a bump and latched tightly together so that the lander crew could climb back into the Command Module for the return trip to earth.

A simulator was built that moved the two full-sized spacecraft in response to their control systems just as they would move in orbit. This simulator not only trained the astronauts to perform the docking maneuver, but also checked out the control systems and the mechanism that latched the two vehicles together.

The lunar landing was the other extremely important maneuver. The Lunar Lander was equipped with an automatic radar-controlled landing system that could make the touchdown without human help. But the pilot had to be able to take over if that system malfunctioned, or if the pilot saw that the automatic landing was going to take place in an area that was too rough. And indeed, that is exactly what happened on the first Apollo moon landing—Astronaut Neil Armstrong saw that the Lander was headed into a field of boulders, and took control to move to a smoother site and make the touchdown himself.

The Lunar Lander was a new kind of vehicle, in that it rode down to a landing on the airless moon solely by the thrust of its rockets. Because it landed straight down and took off straight up, the Lander flew more like a helicopter than an airplane. The astronauts received training in helicopters and in a special vehicle that was lifted into the air by downward-pointed jet engines. But the most important device for training pilots for the lunar landing was a simulator that was a perfect replica of the Lunar Module cabin, with a simulated out-the-window view of the moon's surface.

This simulator operated much like the airplane simulators described in earlier chapters—it could pretend that it was a Lunar Module actually descending to a touchdown on the moon. Each switch and control gave a command to a computer that calculated what the Landing Module would do, and the panel instruments showed the pilot his attitude, speed, rate of descent,

Inside this "box," lunar mission astronauts practiced landing on the moon hundreds of times while still here on earth.

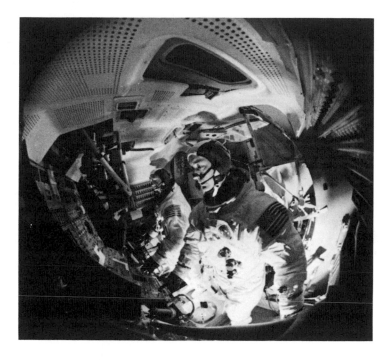

A "fish-eye" camera view of the inside of the lunar module mission simulator. Astronauts Neil Armstrong (*left*) and Michael Collins (*right*) work the controls.

and other needed information. The computer kept track of all vital information, such as the amount of fuel used in the landing and the amount left for takeoff for the return trip back to earth. This was something the pilot had to watch carefully, because if the landing used fuel that would be needed for takeoff, the crew would not get back from the moon. The computer also moved the lunar scene outside the window so that the pilot could visually judge the distance from the surface and land on it.

The performance of the Lander's controls was also investigated in the simulator and used to modify the controls to help the pilots to make the best possible landings. With the Lunar Landing Simulator, astronauts could make as many as fifty moon landings a day, in perfect safety. It was this kind of training that made the lunar missions such a success.

The centerpiece of the Apollo program was the full-mission simulator. This simulator consisted of complete working mock-ups of the Command Module and Lunar Lander cabins, in which nearly all switches, controls, and gauges worked just as they did on the real spacecraft. As in the aircraft simulators, the astronauts were flying a computer that calculated what the spacecraft, or any of its systems, would do, and gave the crew the information they needed on the instrument panel.

Even the stars in the sky were simulated in the view out the window. This simulation was so accurate that the crew could take a navigation sight on the stars at any point in the mission, and find out exactly where they were "in space."

The shape of the simulator is confusing, because you can scarcely see the spacecraft modules among all the odd-shaped boxes that lie at all angles to each other. These boxes house the star-projection system and other components. The astronauts nicknamed this simulator "the train wreck," and indeed it looked a little like a pile-up of railroad boxcars.

For full-mission simulations, the Apollo simulator was hooked up to launch control at Cape Kennedy, to Mission Control in Houston, and to the network of other tracking stations around the world. With all crews and controllers in place, the complete countdown of the

The Apollo Mission Simulator (the "train wreck") in the background is programmed by instructors at the panel below. Astronauts "fly" the mission in mockups of the two module cabins just as they would on the space mission.

launching rocket was simulated, after which the flight was handed over to Mission Control.

Numerous computers simulated the flight in every detail. The astronauts could read what they needed on the gauges, which showed such things as fuel and oxygen remaining, the importance of which will be described in the next chapter. The crew operated the spacecraft's systems, took sightings on the stars, fired the rockets for mid-course corrections, and did all the things that they would do on a real mission.

The simulator had a speed-up feature by which the clock could be speeded up for long parts of the three-day flight out to the moon during which not very much happens. By putting the simulator into "fast-forward," a mission requiring many days could be compressed into hours. As with all modern simulators, the action could be stopped at any point, or returned to repeat some activity that was done incorrectly or needed to be practiced again.

By the time space crews traveled to the moon, their spacecraft, its controls, and the flight itself were all very familiar. They had looked back at the amazing sight of the receding earth and ahead at the approaching moon many times from the windows of the simulator. When the lunar module pilot made his approach and landing on the real lunar surface, he used the skill acquired by doing it hundreds of times in the safety of the simulator back on earth a quarter of a million miles away.

THE SPACE
SHUTTLE SIMULATOR

The spaceflight simulators used by NASA have shown that simulators are vital to space missions, and will likely

Crew for Space Shuttle Mission STS-27
assemble for a training session on the
flight deck of the Shuttle Mission Simulator.

be built for all future space missions. The new space shuttle simulator is the latest addition to the fleet.

This simulator is in some ways a combination of a spacecraft simulator and a large-airplane simulator. The shuttle is boosted into orbit by huge rockets as well as its own rocket engines, flies like a spacecraft while in the vacuum of space, and becomes, after reentry, an unpowered airplane that must be flown with great precision to a gliderlike landing on an airport runway. An array of part-task trainers prepares the shuttle astronauts for the vast instrument panels of the shuttle. A full simulator has—like the Mercury, Gemini and Apollo simulators—communication links to launch control and Mission Control to give both space crews and ground controllers the experience and practice of a full shuttle mission.

The spaceflight simulators are so versatile that they are sometimes used for duties hardly expected by their designers. For example, on the *Apollo 13* mission, the third flight launched for a landing on the moon's surface, a serious accident occurred when the spacecraft was 180,000 miles away, still hurtling away from earth at 2,000 miles per hour, and quite unable to turn back. The story of the rescue of *Apollo 13* in 1970, and of the part played by the Apollo Mission Simulator, is told in the next chapter.

EIGHT

UNLUCKY APOLLO 13

"Hey, we've got a problem here!"

A startled Mission Control shot back: "This is Houston; say again please."

"Houston we've had a problem. . . . we've had a [power interruption] and a pretty large bang associated with the warning."

This terse radio message from 180,000 miles out in space alerted Mission Control that an accident had happened to the *Apollo 13* spacecraft on its way to the moon—a serious accident from which the astronaut crew would be rescued with the help of simulators here on earth.

Both Mission Control in Houston and the astronaut crew aboard the Command Module sprang into action on reviewing emergency checklists, reading gauges, throwing switches, while questions and answers crackled back and forth on the radio. The hatch between the Command Module (CM) and the Lunar Module (LM) was slammed shut in case something was wrong in the LM.

The crew reported that they could see through the window particles and vapors of some kind that indicated their spacecraft was "venting" into space. Because gas leaking anywhere out of the spacecraft acts like a small rocket, the spacecraft also was beginning to tumble.

What had happened? The crew would not know for some time, but action had to be taken immediately to prevent any unnecessary use or loss of oxygen, electrical power, fuel, and water. Without enough of these vital supplies, a safe return to earth would be unlikely, perhaps impossible.

The Apollo mission vehicle (consisting of the Command Module, Service Module, and Lunar Module— Figure 4), already more than two days out into space, hurtled still farther away from earth as the technical specialists for each of the spacecraft systems pored over their manuals. Slowly the answers came. The pressure in an oxygen tank in the Service Module had risen rapidly, then suddenly dropped to zero. Had the tank exploded, sprung a large leak, been punctured by a meteorite strike, or what? No one knew. Within two hours a second oxygen tank showed "empty," and two fuel cells were no longer producing electrical power. It was clear that no moon landing would be possible. The mission would have to be aborted. All efforts had to be made to get the crew safely back to earth as quickly as possible.

The problem was that the spacecraft was still moving away from earth at nearly 2,200 miles per hour. (The spacecraft had lost much of its original speed because it was coasting "uphill," that is, against the pull of earth's gravity.) It could not simply turn around and return; there was not enough rocket fuel available to safely make such a maneuver. The only practical way to return would

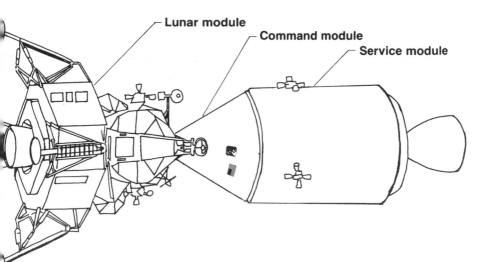

Lunar module

Command module

Service module

Figure 4. On its way to the moon, the Apollo Command Module was nose-to-nose with the Lunar Module, so the crew could move from one to the other via the "tunnel." The unoccupied Service Module contained fuel, other supplies, and small rocket engines. Only the Command Module returned to earth.

be to continue toward the moon and use the moon's gravity to swing the spacecraft out around the moon and fling it back toward earth. A couple of short bursts of rocket thrust for small course corrections would be necessary, and it seemed likely that there would be enough rocket fuel and electrical power available for this.

But the spacecraft, with its precious cargo of three astronauts, still had to fly for three or four more days through the vacuum of space. In previous earth-orbit programs, Mercury and Gemini, the spacecraft had never been more than 100 miles or 20 minutes from earth, and never more than about an hour and a half from a recovery ship. The Apollo moon mission had long been recognized as a much more dangerous project; space crews would fly a quarter of a million miles into space, and would then be several *days* from a possible touchdown on earth.

After this explosion, or whatever it was, aboard *Apollo 13,* would there be enough oxygen, electrical power, water, and other consumables to keep the crew alive long enough to get back to earth? How could Mission Control find out quickly? How could the controllers or crew compare all the possible ways of using and conserving the onboard supplies, and plan the return flight path that would have the best chance for success?

The answer: use the Apollo full-mission simulator. The simulator, like a giant computer, was already programmed to respond to any maneuver, any flight plan, any change in procedure, and show the simulator crew and the engineers of Mission Control just what would happen to the real spacecraft.

Within a very short time of the accident, the Apollo simulators at Mission Control in Houston, at the Kennedy Spaceflight Center, and at the spacecraft manufacturer's plant were manned by skilled astronaut and engineer crews around the clock. With the simulator directed to pretend that it was the wounded spacecraft, the crews flew and reflew various parts of the mission— probing, experimenting, checking out procedures that might be used to save the lives of their comrades out in space. If one procedure used too much oxygen or fuel or electrical power, it was abandoned and others were tried.

The Lunar Module had long been counted on for emergency use in case of a serious failure or shortage of supplies in the Command Module during flight. Designed to be crashed into the surface of the moon (after it had returned the astronauts from the lunar surface to the Command Module) the LM did not have the heat protection it needed to get safely back through the fiery reentry into earth's atmosphere. But with its vital supplies of oxygen, electrical power, and fuel, it could serve as a "lifeboat" during the long trip homeward through airless space. Having done this job, it would be abandoned near earth, along with the Service Module. Instead of smashing to bits on the moon's surface, both would burn up from friction as they plunged into the earth's atmosphere.

Now that the *Apollo 13* crew knew that the LM had not been damaged in the explosion, the hatch between the LM and the Command Module was opened once again. Crew members moved into the Lunar Module to ready it for its new duties as a lifeboat. To conserve power, it was decided that only one life-support system in the two modules would be operated at any one time; consequently, a duct was needed to carry fresh oxygen from the LM to the Command Module. A makeshift duct was pasted up in the simulator using paper and cardboard from flight manuals, and instructions sent up by radio for doing the same aboard the Command Module.

At launch, *Apollo 13* had been carefully rocketed onto a path that would bring it into lunar orbit sixty miles above the surface, from which the descent to lunar landing would begin. Now this path was changed with a short rocket burn to a free-return path. On this flight path the spacecraft would pass close enough to the moon so that the moon's gravity would swing it around the moon and hurl it back to earth, even if no further rocket thrust was available. The splashdown point would be in the Indian Ocean, some ninety hours (nearly four days!) away.

Although it was now certain that the spacecraft would return to earth, there were still several problems. First, because the Lunar Module was returning to earth instead of being crashed onto the moon, new procedures for making course corrections and for jettisoning this module near earth had to be developed. Second, the consumables—oxygen, water and power—aboard the spacecraft would be dangerously low by reentry time. And third, only a few recovery ships were available in this general area to pick the spacecraft out of the ocean. Another small course correction later—if it could be made—would put splashdown in a better place in a shorter time.

Half a day later, the spacecraft arrived near the moon, where the moon's gravity swung it around the moon and hurled it back toward earth. As the ship left the vicinity of the moon, another rocket burn that had been worked out in the simulators was attempted. This course correction was successful, and moved the splashdown point to the South Pacific, about half a day earlier.

After this maneuver only one question remained: Did the spacecraft have enough oxygen, water, and electric power (for heat) to keep the crew alive? In an all-out effort to conserve onboard supplies, spacecraft systems had been shut down to only those absolutely required to support the crew. For two days, the crews in the simulators wrestled with this question.

"We've tried to simulate virtually everything that we've had the crew do that is non-normal," said a spokesman for Mission Control, "and we've proven most everything that we've been able to run on the simulator prior to passing it up to them."

The answers gathered from the simulators were reassuring: barring unforeseen problems, the Apollo crew should make it back safely.

The simulators also checked out the method of jettisoning the Service Module first, then the Lunar Module—reverse order from other flights. These maneuvers had to be done correctly, so that the jettisoned modules would move safely away from the Command Module with no danger of future collisions.

It grew cold in the crew quarters, as low as 43°F at times. One day before reentry, the crew found that no water could be drawn from the CM tank, and it was assumed to be empty. An inspection after landing showed that there was plenty of water in the tank; apparently ice had blocked the pipes. Condensation fogged the windows of the spacecraft for most of the flight, and interfered with navigation shots of the stars. But in general, the crew was reasonably comfortable.

Five hours before reentry a final small course correction was performed with a short rocket burn. The Service Module, containing rocket engines and supplies that were no longer needed, was then separated from the Command Module. As the damaged SM drifted away, the crew in the Command Module got their only chance to photograph the damaged area. From eighty feet away, the crew could see that a hole had been blown in the side of the Service Module from which insulation was hanging out. (Later laboratory tests and analysis of data showed that the oxygen tank had exploded in the SM.)

The Lunar Module was kept attached as long as possible, in order to keep using its oxygen and electrical power. Its batteries were drained to bring those in the

Command Module up to full charge. Then the LM was jettisoned by disconnecting it and allowing the air pressure in the tunnel between the two space vehicles to "pop" the two apart. The astronauts watched with some sadness as the Lunar Module drifted away. The LM "lifeboat" had helped to save their lives, but was not equipped for the plunge into the earth's atmosphere. It would not survive reentry, except perhaps for some scorched scraps of metal that would fall into the south Pacific Ocean where, as someone in Mission Control said, "the water is nice and deep."

The reentry of the Command Module was routine, as was the landing in open sea between Samoa and New Zealand. The recovery crews were ready in the target area, and the astronauts were aboard the recovery ship within forty-five minutes of splashdown.

Six thousand miles away, the simulators that had been so vital in the task of bringing the crew back safely were shut down. They sat in their laboratories, dark and empty, waiting for their next mission.

NINE

SIMULATORS GO TO SEA

Imagine yourself the captain of a huge ocean vessel, one of the largest, heaviest machines that moves around on the surface of this planet. Standing in the bridge, or control room, of such a vessel, what would you need to know in order to be able to operate it safely?

First, you would need a thorough understanding of how all the controls, switches, indicators, navigation systems, and propulsion systems work. Next, you would need to experience for yourself just how the mammoth ship handles—how long it takes to speed up or slow down, how much space it needs to maneuver.

Freight and passenger ships, for example, may weigh from a few hundred tons to the 66,000 tons of the 1000-foot luxury liner *Queen Elizabeth II* (QE II). Even this ship is dwarfed by the supertankers of half a million tons and more.

Although they have propulsion engines of great power, the great weight of these ships makes it impossible to bring them up to speed or stop them quickly.

For example, many miles are needed for the ship's 200,000 horsepower to bring the QE II up to its cruising speed of 28 knots. Even with power completely shut off and the tremendous amount of water resistance on the hull, the great heavy weight of the ship would keep it plowing ahead for miles before it stopped.

Ships also operate, as do airplanes, when fog or darkness limit visibility. To move safely across the ocean or in crowded ports, ships carry an assortment of electronic gear to help their crews navigate, avoid colliding with other ships, or keep from running aground. Some of their navigational radio systems use signals from shore stations, others use signals from satellites orbiting the earth. Several different kinds of radar devices help sort out other ships, buoys, and landmarks, while depth sounders probe the depth and shape of the sea bottom.

Although a trainee can learn a great deal by observing and working with an experienced crew at sea, it would take a long time to acquire the wide range of experiences that might be encountered. A foggy arrival in Amsterdam harbor, or a sudden shutdown of engines in the crowded port of Singapore, might not occur to show the trainee "what it's like," or how to handle such an emergency.

RADAR
SIMULATORS

Specialized simulators have been built to train ship officers in the use of basic radar equipment, which is aboard every ship in use today. The trainee stands at an actual radar console which can be programmed to sim-

Two trainees stand over their radarscopes
to solve a collision-avoidance problem in
a radar simulator. A computer moves
the radar "targets"—and the trainees'
ship—as programmed by the instructor.

ulate open sea or a variety of worldwide harbor areas—from Rotterdam to Yokahama. Indicators and controls on the console include instruments showing heading and speed, a telegraph used to communicate with the engine room, rudder control, gyropilot commands, and plotting table adjacent to the radarscope.

For whatever lesson is planned, channels, buoys, land, and radio transmitting stations are shown on the radarscope exactly as they would be at the real location. The student's task is to observe and identify the blips on the radarscope, swiftly and accurately analyze the direction and speed of other ships, plot their courses, and decide whether they pose any collision hazard. The student can then change course, or telegraph power and speed change requests to the engine room.

The displays and images on the radarscope and other instruments are, of course, all generated by the simulator's computers. But to the student behind the closed curtain, it's the same as being truly alone at the radar set on the high seas.

The instructor can give the trainee a variety of problems to be solved. The instructor can program one or more target ships of varying sizes, speeds, and maneuverability for the trainee to interpret. Sea conditions, including current speed and direction, wind, and wave size can also be punched into the simulator's computer by the instructor.

When the student finally arrives in a real ship for the first time at, for example, busy Yokahama harbor, he may very well have seen almost anything that could happen during earlier simulator training. Simulator training on basic radar equipment is essential for crews, enabling them to be able to avoid collisions when operating their ships in crowded coastal and harbor areas, or on the high seas.

COLLISION
AVOIDANCE RADAR
SYSTEMS (CARS)

More recent advancements in radar technology have enabled many ship owners to install sophisticated Collision Avoidance Radar Systems (nicknamed CARS). This newer gear is really a computerized radar, which will detect, plot, and analyze any target's course and speed; compare this course with the ship's track; and predict whether a collision would take place, and when.

The simulator looks very similar to other radarscopes, except that the operator does not manually compute the information needed. Instead, a computer does all the arithmetic and gives the operator the answer.

Instead of manually plotting courses of blips or targets on a basic radarscope, the operator uses a joy stick to select targets on his scope that appear to be on a threatening course to the ship. With a target selected, the radar's computer then calculates its speed and course, and looks for the possibility of collision. If one appears likely, the computerized radar then recommends a course and speed change for the ship.

To simulate what might happen in a crowded sea lane, the instructor may scatter a dozen targets across the screen for the student to sort out and make decisions about in order to avoid collisions. In case one type of radar fails, many ships have both the basic radar and the computerized versions. Deck officers of large ships become knowledgeable and comfortable with both types through the extensive use of simulators, long before they try operating the equipment while standing on their sea legs.

NAVIGATION AND
SHIP PROPULSION
PLANT SIMULATORS

Other equipment that maritime students may learn to operate through use of simulators include satellite navigation systems (SATNAV), navigation by shore radio beacons (*LOng RAnge Navigation*, or LORAN), Radio Direction Finding (RDF), and operation of a depth sounder, a device which constantly measures the depth of the water below the ship's hull. Using part-task simulators for these individual systems, students learn to tune, identify, and interpret signals generated by the computer or by the instructor, and use that information for navigating the "ship."

Much of what makes a large ship run is controlled below decks in the engine room. Apart from the huge propulsion engines, engineering officers are also responsible for all the other systems needed to operate the ship—electric power generation, compressed air systems, fuel oil and lubrication systems, water distillation systems, and sewage systems, to name a few.

Engine control room simulators are used by both deck and engineering officers to learn to operate these complex systems efficiently and to identify and solve problems when they occur. Trainees have not only a complete mock-up of the entire engine room control panel, but also a pictorial display board which uses colored lights and animation to demonstrate how a system operates.

This simulator mimics the control center for the propulsion, steering, electrical, and other vital systems for a whole ship. Simulator's computer shows the result of each operation on panel instruments and on the lighted system diagram.

SHIP'S BRIDGE
SIMULATORS

A ship's bridge is the control center of the ship. In this spacious room overlooking the forward deck of the ship are the radar and navigational equipment, radio communications and signaling gear, steering and autopilot equipment, and engine room controls. Here also are the people who use this equipment, as a team under the captain, to keep the ship running safely, day and night, from port to port.

Many of these people have learned to operate their particular gear in simulators, and many are trained to operate more than one piece of equipment. Their training into the team on the ship's bridge is widely done on the job, working at sea under the supervision of experienced crew members. But training for such duty, like many others described in this book, is also performed in simulators. In the full bridge simulator, as many as fifteen students at one time can participate in the operation of the ship, sharing and coordinating duties under the captain's supervision.

The simulator consists of a complete mock-up of a ship's bridge. Through the window, instead of the ocean, is a computer-generated view of the harbor or coast, with channel markers, buoys, and other ships all in place. As in other simulators, these visual effects are generated either by television equipment or by computer.

The computer takes the control motions by the crew and "moves" the ship, generates the harbor view, and controls the instruments with near-perfect reproduction of an actual ship. All controls, steering wheel, instruments, radar systems, and communication stations are

Ship's Bridge Simulator can train the whole bridge
crew at once for all the tasks of operating a ship. Seen
through the windows is a simulated view of the harbor
or sea, along with buoys, other ships, and navigation aids.

fully operative. All the simulator's systems—propulsion, boiler, electrical, navigation, and so on—respond to control movements as exactly as would those of a real ship.

Problems or emergencies, a ship or buoy in the way for example, can be programmed by the instructor. As in the case of the airline simulator, the captain and his team can improve their decision-making skills and practice emergency drills required for licensed deck officers, without ever going to sea!

Let's look at a typical lesson for a crew being qualified on a large tanker. The instructor has called up the computer-stored profile for the Atlantic approach to the Panama Canal, and the exercise begins with the crew maneuvering in preparation for transit through the waterway. The area is highly congested with other ships. The crew uses the collision avoidance radar to plot courses, and the captain issues commands to the helm accordingly. All telegraph and radio messages are received and transmitted just as if the "ship" were in Panama.

The instructor, at his own console, arranges for a ship out ahead to change course suddenly and steam full ahead across the path of the training ship. Alarms go off on the radar sets to alert the crew of a possible collision. Unimportant radio messages from "shore" (the instructor) try to distract and overload the crew during this critical time. A rainstorm cuts the visibility out the forward window to near zero. As if that's not enough, engine sensors reveal an impending propulsion failure. As the instructor "fails" the engine on the ship, the crew attempts to carry out the captain's order to drop anchor, only to find that the anchor is jammed. A slight improvement in the weather shows glimpses of the span of the bridge the huge ship is now drifting dangerously toward . . . and so on.

Such an exercise, while perhaps exaggerated, could very well have been taken from the logs or accident reports of a real operation. The emergencies re-enacted in the simulator test the crew's ability to operate their equipment, make good decisions, and avert disaster at sea. Videos of the exercise can later be discussed in arm-chair comfort with no risk whatever to lives or equipment.

SHIP-LOADING
SIMULATORS

It is just as easy for a ship to be damaged or sunk while standing at its pier as it is while moving at sea or in the harbor. The cargo that a ship takes into its hold weighs many times as much as the empty hull. The cargo must be properly loaded into the various tanks or holds of the ship in the proper sequence if the vessel is to balance and float properly. Discharge or unloading at the ship's destination is just as important. Improper order of loading or unloading of either liquid or bulk cargo can produce stresses that can buckle a bulkhead, bend the frame, or "break the back" of a steel ship!

The value of cargo carried in large tankers is very great, and the economic loss from contaminating or mixing grades of cargo or contaminating the sea with oil can be extremely high. Thus, loading operations require careful planning and a high level of skill. Although ship crews can be trained on the job in real ships, simulators provide a means of training quickly, safely, and efficiently on shore.

The ship-loading simulator generally consists of a

Crew members responsible for loading their ship learn how to do it safely in this ship-loading simulator. Lighted pictorial display at top shows consequence of actions taken on the cargo- and ballast-loading control panel below.

full mock-up panel containing all the pump switches and valves, as well as diagrams of the tanks and compartments of a ship's hold. The simulator accepts the loading performed by the trainee, then calculates and gives back to the trainee critical measurements such as center of gravity, center of flotation, displacement, bending and sagging deflection of the hull, and ship trim. As with other simulators, failures and emergencies in the loading process can be simulated to train ship officers to handle such events.

MODEL SHIPS
THAT SIMULATE

One type of ship simulator looks like a fun ride at an amusement park. But, in fact, it is used for the very serious business of training ship captains and officers. This simulator does its job in a different and interesting way—in real water, with real current, wind, and waves.

The actual feel of a heavy ship in motion under real conditions cannot be adequately duplicated with the stationary black box electronic simulators we've discussed. For some training, there is still the need to feel and see the effects of running a ponderous, heavy ship in real water, current, wind, and wave conditions. Because ships have a huge mass, even a "bump" against a pier can cause serious damage. Although perfect simulation of all conditions is not possible, the effects of weight and motion can be better felt and seen through use of these model ships.

Captains come from all over the world to climb aboard more than a dozen model ships of various sizes and weights at Port Revel in remote central France. The models are exact scale replicas of real ships, but twenty-five times smaller. Even what the trainee sees of the ship, water, and horizon has been simulated by having the trainee seated with eye position on the model "bridge" at exactly the same place it would be on the real ship.

The model ship must not only look like the real ship, but more importantly, it must move and feel like it as well. To simulate the reactions of the full-scale ship, each model has heavy weights in the proper place to simulate the load of the real ship. These iron weights are removable so that varying loads can be simulated, from empty to maximum cargo.

The response of model ships to sea or weather conditions, to propeller thrust, and to rudder movement, is as close as possible to that of the real ship. With any power setting, the model ship must accelerate to the correct speed in the correct distance, in proportion to its size. It must also perform a turn with a given rudder setting at the correct (scale) radius of turn. Wave-making and current-making machinery can be switched on in the middle of the lake, to simulate waves in the open sea to a height of 20 feet.

The model ships are driven by battery-operated electric motors, which reproduce "scale" thrust through both stern propellers and bow thrusters. The controls and indicators appear on the model's bridge, just as on the actual vessel. These sea captains are *not* scooting around in model speed boats, but lumbering and slosh-ing around in heavy, slow, clumsy little model ships that act and feel much like the big ships they simulate.

Once familiar with how the model ship handles, the ship captains go to work practicing techniques in this tiny pond which they may need to know later when in full-size ships on the open ocean. They maneuver in shallow water, in narrow channels, ship canals, and locks. They practice bringing ships or different cargoes and weights into all types of berths or anchorages. Two or more ships can practice overtaking or passing in a ship canal, or coming alongside one another, as two tankers might do in the open ocean to transfer crude oil loads while under way.

During another lesson, the student might practice anchoring. Not only are the anchors on the model ships to scale, but the chain size, the holding power, and the point at which overloaded anchor lines will break are also to scale. One of the more difficult maneuvers is the approach and tie-up to an offshore oil rig.

Instructors in a small outboard motorboat follow the students in the model ships, since there is no room in the models for extra people. So that the trainee and instructor can look back over particular maneuvers, a track recording system is used to follow the water models under way. A nearby tower receives infrared signals from tiny transmitters in each model on the lake. A computer records information about the model—speed and heading, wind speed, propeller speeds, even the angle on the rudder used to steer the ship. A printout of this information is used later to show the student's exact track through the water, and what position the controls were in during certain maneuvers.

This unique training facility offers ship officers valuable practice in some of the more difficult maneuvers of ship handling. Model ship simulators are very different from the other kinds of simulators, in that they use small models that can pretend they are big ships. When used in tandem with the electronic simulators, these model simulators can cover virtually all facets of safe ship handling.

TEN

INDUSTRIAL SIMULATORS

Industrial operations such as chemical plants and oil refineries involve a large number of processes. Raw materials enter at one point and flow through the various processing stations, finally emerging as finished products. Raw crude oil, for example, enters a refinery from storage tanks or a pipeline, and after a series of many processes on its way through the plant, finally emerges as gasoline, fuel oil, kerosene, and other products.

Such plants often have central control stations. A large, elaborate panel is built on a diagram of the processing plant, with indicating lights, gauges, switches, alarms, and other controls shown in their proper locations. From such a panel, technicians may control hundreds of operations over many acres of plant equipment. Despite the use of automatic controls and safety precautions, a skilled operator is needed to monitor the various processes, handle emergencies, and see that the plant runs smoothly. Even a small oversight or mistake could contaminate or spoil a large quantity of expensive material, or probably cause damage or danger to the machinery and the plant.

Although new operators can be trained on the job by learning from experienced technicians, such training has disadvantages. It tends to distract the operators, and the trainee is an extra hand who must be paid while in training. More important, it may take a long time to teach a new trainee all that he or she needs to know, especially how to deal with emergencies.

Simulators offer a safer, cheaper, easier way to train operating personnel in process industries. The simulator may consist of a duplicate of the plant's control panel, with a large, lighted diagram of the plant, and all the controls and indicators in their proper places. These controls are not connected to valves and pumps and boilers, but to a computer that can pretend it is the refinery or chemical plant. The computer calculates what the trainee's actions on the panel would do in the actual plant, and shows him or her the results on the panel gauges and lights and also on the instructor's panel.

The instructor can program problems and emergencies with which the trainee must be able to deal. The instructor can then evaluate the trainee's ability to cope with these problems.

At the simulator, the trainee can learn the job quickly and safely. He or she can experience an array of "emergencies" that might be met only after many years of service in the real plant. The trainee can make mistakes, too—blow a safety valve, overheat a process, burn out a pump, run a tank dry, cause a fire—all in complete safety.

NUCLEAR
POWER PLANT
SIMULATORS

The control panel of a nuclear power plant such as the Commanche Peak plant in Texas is a large array of diagrams, lights, instruments, controls and alarms. Because of the enormous amount of energy being converted from heat into electrical power, a nuclear power plant must be designed for maximum safety and with multiple backup systems. If one important unit—such as a pump or valve—fails, another takes over automatically. If the second one fails, there may be another

Simulator panel for the Commanche Peak nuclear power plant in Texas is a duplicate of the real thing. The student-operator tends the panel, while the instructor programs his problems at the panel in the foreground. A computer plays the part of the power plant.

backup to take over, if the function is a vital one. All the safety and backup systems make the whole plant very complex. Although the plant is equipped with many automatic systems that can ordinarily do a better job than a human operator, these systems must be carefully monitored by an operator who must still make decisions and take action when necessary. A nuclear power plant uses complicated and lengthy start-up and shutdown procedures that also require skilled operators.

Although new power-plant operators are still trained in classrooms and on the job, simulators have taken over much of the training. Besides training new operators, simulators are used to give experienced operators periodic refresher training to be certain that they are still fully qualified, not only for routine operation but for any emergencies that may occur.

RAILROAD
SIMULATORS

Railroad locomotive engineers have a fast-moving job in heavy vehicles with special operational problems: speed limits, signal-controlled stops and starts, and very long starting and stopping distances. Moving along the tracks at 50 to 60 miles per hour while pulling a string of 150 heavy freight cars is hardly the place to discuss or demonstrate to a trainee the dangers of a warning light or switch signal. However, it would be too expensive to assemble a practice train to ride the rails so that new engineers would be able to experience firsthand how a train feels from the locomotive's cab. A railroad simulator is one more example of how the safe operation of a large vehicle can be better learned without actually using the real thing.

Student locomotive engineer operates this locomotive simulator down tracks by signals seen through his window.

The railroad simulator is a full-scale mock-up of a modern diesel locomotive cab. Like the aircraft cockpit, it is fitted with a set of controls identical to that of a real locomotive, with gauges, throttle, brakes, speed indicators, alarms, and switches. Even the sounds and sensations of train operation are simulated to add realism.

Trainee railroad engineers see out the simulator window either a video film or computer-generated images of exactly what an engineer sees during an actual run. The film sequences can depict simply routine main line operation, or they can take the trainee through traffic, problem crossings, terminals, or complex switch yards. Trainees can learn or review what different signals mean and how to comply, and how to deal with meeting and passing other trains. Emergency stops or other procedures that would be far too hazardous to practice during an actual run down the tracks can be experienced safely in the simulator.

AIR TRAFFIC
CONTROL SIMULATION

The air traffic controller's task is to assign a block of air space to each aircraft departing from or arriving at a terminal area or traveling on en route airways. To keep aircraft separated, controllers assign each aircraft directional headings, routes, and altitudes to follow. Using radar, controllers watch the aircraft, shown only as blips on their screens. By two-way radio, controllers sort out dozens of aircraft, and give precise instructions to pilots.

A controller must learn to do an incredible number of tasks at one time. In addition to keeping a dozen or more aircraft safely separated, a controller may need to space them properly for landing, one after another. During bad weather, the controller may have to stack the aircraft in a holding pattern, all circling in the murk, separated by a thousand feet of altitude while they wait their turn to approach for a landing. If an aircraft has an emergency during this process—an engine failure, a pressurization problem, a heart attack victim on board—the controller must give priority to the distress call, and thread the emergency aircraft through the thick of other aircraft to a safe landing.

The air traffic control simulator is essentially a duplicate of the controllers' stations, complete with radarscopes, radio microphones, and headsets, and panels of switches operating the various pieces of equipment at the controller's console. As in other simulators, computers behind the scene and instructors at their console make the simulator pretend that it is a unit of the air traffic control system.

Trainees first learn to identify, track, communicate with, and control aircraft blips that move across their radarscopes. The instructor gradually increases the number of aircraft to be handled, first two or three, and finally a dozen or more, to simulate a controller's ultimate workload. The controller trainee can also practice the other skills required to become a qualified controller: assigning blocks of air space, routing aircraft, and handling emergencies. Simulators help to train operators safely and quickly for both routine tasks and emergencies that they may encounter in their complex jobs.

ELEVEN

THE FUTURE:
THE WORLD IN A "BOX"?

Ed Link's first simulator was originally conceived as a device that could train airplane pilots more cheaply than in an actual airplane. From it has grown a family of devices that provides not just a cheaper way to train aircraft pilots and operators of complex equipment, but the *only* way to train them to handle dangerous emergencies. Engine failure in an airliner, a missile attack on enemy aircraft by a supersonic fighter, near-collisions of ships in crowded harbors, spacecraft landings on the moon, and loss-of-cooling incidents in nuclear power plants are all critical emergencies that must be practiced by operators of these machines.

These dangerous situations cannot be practiced in the real machines without great cost and unacceptable risk. The simulator, which can pretend with almost perfect realism that it is an airplane streaking through the night sky, or a ship plowing through harbor fog, or a spacecraft landing among lunar boulders, can train the operator to the high degree of skill he needs with no risk whatever.

The modern simulator could never have been developed if the technology had been limited to mechanical push-rods, electrical relays, and air bellows from the organ business. Simulating a complex machine of today, such as an airliner, a supersonic fighter, or a spaceship, requires thousands of complex calculations to be made and repeated over and over again at high speed. It was the development of the high-speed electronic computer that brought the simulator into full bloom.

The electronic computer has also made possible a new kind of simulation that is used not to train operators, but to simulate a particular process. In such a "computer simulation" a system is broken down into its separate processes, and mathematical equations are developed to describe each process and the interrelations among them.

For example, the weather over the United States is such a system. The weather bureau has a network of stations that measure atmospheric conditions at frequent intervals around the clock, both on the ground and at various altitudes. Measurements of local conditions such as temperature, pressure, moisture content, and wind are made and fed into a central computer. Using equations that can predict what will happen to each mass of air as it moves about and interacts with other masses, the computer can make the millions of calculations needed to predict the weather for locations all around the country.

Computer simulation is being used to explore war situations; traffic on railroads, on highways, and in the air; and to test chemical plant processes long before a plant is built. It is being used to study the effects of pollutants on ecological systems, such as the effect of acid rain on lakes and forests. The operation of energy systems, including networks of long-distance, high-voltage power lines, is studied in this way. Studies of the human body by computer simulation are providing new information on the effects of both physiological and environmental stress. Nearly everything in the world can be studied by computer simulation.

Perhaps the crowning achievement will be the simulation of the whole world, all at once, in a computer. A move toward such a project was begun in 1968 with the formation of a group of economists, industrialists, scientists, planners, educators, and others, that called itself the Club of Rome. The founder of the group, an internationally known Italian economist and businessman named Aurelio Peccei, summarized his views and his analysis in an article published in 1971.

The world, he said, is heading toward large-scale ecological, political, and social disorders. The threats are global, and overarch humanity's national, ideological and racial divisions. We must, he indicated, start with a reasonably good knowledge of the present and explore the interaction of the ever-changing problems that make our future unstable and uncertain.

The Club commissioned the Massachusetts Institute of Technology (MIT) in 1970 to develop a set of simulation models of the world. The models took into account such factors as global population growth, pollution, food production, natural resource depletion, and economic development. Data on these elements, along with equations representing the interrelationships of these factors, were fed into a computer. The computer was asked to simulate the coming changes and the future of the world.

The results were shocking. They showed, according to the Club of Rome, that there is "absolutely no possibility" the world can long support the present growth of population. Pollution, depletion of resources, and other problems have already gone so far that the quality of life on earth is on a downward slide that might be unstoppable.

A startled scientific community sprang into action, and more computer simulations were made. Other groups soon disputed the Club of Rome's calculations, and argued that the simulation needed to be refined. Perhaps the world situation is not quite as grim as the original simulation had shown. Doom, in other words, may not be quite so close upon us.

This study also illustrates that the output of the computer simulation—and indeed any of the simulators we have examined in this book—will be only as good as the data and the equations put into it. The computer can neither make judgments nor compensate for bad data or poor instructions. It cannot yield answers that are more accurate or more reliable than the inputs it receives. (Computer specialists have a terse phrase for the consequences of poor input to a computer: "Garbage in, garbage out.")

Although the initial results of the Club of Rome computer simulation may be regarded as preliminary and subject to refinement, the simulation drew worldwide attention to the seriousness of our planet's growing environmental and social problems. It also showed that computer simulation might help to avert world disaster.

Perhaps we shall learn from subsequent simulations what must be done in order to preserve our world and the quality of life upon it. It would be impossible to design and conduct such an experiment in the real world. But we can do it sensibly and safely in a simulator that can pretend it is the world.

GLOSSARY

The definitions in this glossary pertain mainly to their use in this book. More general definitions can be found in unabridged dictionaries.

Air bellows A flexible container of metal, plastic, or other material that can expand and move a load when subjected to inside air pressure.

Airspeed indicator An instrument that senses the pressures of the air passing a moving airplane and indicates the plane's speed through that air.

Altimeter The instrument in an airplane that indicates altitude, as determined by measurement of the pressure of the surrounding air.

Apollo The name given to the American space project to land men on the moon and return them to earth in the 1960s and 1970s.

Approach chart A chart or map depicting routes and procedures for approaching and landing at a particular airport, including all radio and navigational aids.

Backup system Another system that can be used to do the job of a system that has failed.

Black box Technical slang for an electrical or electronic system.

Blip A point of light on a computer screen or radarscope that indicates a target "seen" by the radar.

Box Slang term for simulator. See *Black box.*

Bridge The room or platform above the main deck of a ship from which the ship is controlled.

Capsule In the space program, a term for a space vehicle.

Captain The person in command of an airplane or ship.

Checklist A list of items to be checked and/or set on a control panel before taking a particular action. For example, a takeoff checklist is used by an airplane crew to set all controls and switches for takeoff.

Command Module The Apollo spacecraft module that housed the crew and was the control center for the mission.

Compass (also Magnetic compass) An instrument that senses the magnetic field of the earth and uses it to provide directional information.

Computer-generated image An image (of terrain, sky, other vehicles, etc.) created and moved by a computer and presented to the viewer, as in a simulator.

Data pool The storage area for data in a computer.

Dogfight An aerial battle, especially between fighter aircraft.

Fire-control system A device that uses available inputs, such as radar information, visual sighting, etc., to calculate the aiming of weapons and program their firing.

First officer The person second in command of an airplane; usually the copilot.

Flight engineer The operator of the engineer's panel; the person third in command of an airplane; in some airlines, the second officer.

Flight profile The schedule of altitudes and routes that make up a mission or flight.

Full-mission simulator A simulator in which crews can experience all aspects of a mission.

G refers to the force of gravity. Under a two-G force, one feels a force twice that of gravity.

Gemini The name given to the second American manned space program, which put two astronauts in earth orbit.

Gunship A combat helicopter equipped with guns or other heavy armaments.

Gyroscope A device consisting of a spinning wheel or mass that resists a change in orientation.

High-frequency radio A communication system that uses short-wave, high-frequency radio signals. Example: the common FM radio.

Hydraulic A system in which pressure of a fluid (usually oil) acting on a piston in a cylinder is used to move something. Example: a hydraulic system is used to raise and lower the landing gear of large aircraft.

Instrument flight The operation of an aircraft solely by reference to flight instruments. Requires special license for pilot and, for each flight, a clearance from the air traffic control system.

Low-frequency radio A communication system that uses long-wave, low-frequency radio signals. Example: the common AM radio.

Lunar Module The Apollo spacecraft module that took two astronauts to the surface of the moon, and returned them to the Command Module in lunar orbit.

Mercury The name used for the first American space program to put a man into orbit around the earth in 1961.

Minimum altitude The lowest altitude to which an airplane is allowed to descend in approaching an airport runway when the ground is not visible.

Mock-up A duplicate of a device, such as an airplane cockpit, which resembles, to the degree necessary, the real thing.

Navigator The crew member who uses maps, star sightings, instrument information, etc., to compute position and course during a mission.

Pilot Maker The name given to the first aircraft simulator built by the inventor, Edwin Link.

Pressurization The use of cabin air pressures greater than the pressure outside the aircraft; used in high-altitude flight where the outside air is too thin for comfort or even to sustain life.

Radar An acronym for *RA*dio *D*irection *A*nd *R*anging, a system in which a radio signal is beamed at an object (airplane or ship) and reflected back to the station; measurements of direction and time of transit are used to determine direction and distance from the station.

Retro-rockets Rocket motors used to slow the motion of a spacecraft, especially to cause it to drop into a path for reentry into the earth's atmosphere.

Service Module The unmanned module on the Apollo moon mission that contained batteries, fuel, and other supplies, and a rocket engine.

Simulator A machine that simulates certain conditions or operations for the purpose of training or experimentation.

Software The instructions placed into a computer to program it for a particular task.

Sonar An acronym for *SO*und *N*avigation *A*nd *R*anging; a system for locating and tracking ships (especially submarines) by listening to their sounds, or by bouncing sounds from their hulls.

Speedbrake panels Flaps or panels extended from an airplane, usually the fuselage, to create drag to slow the airplane.

Tank An armored, self-propelled, armed war vehicle.

Throttle The control that governs the speed or power output of an engine.

Thrust reversers Devices at the exit end of a jet engine that scoop up part of the engine-exhaust stream and turn it forward, thus producing reverse thrust to slow the airplane during landing roll-out on the runway after landing.

Tracer A bullet that shows its path by leaving behind a streak of fire or smoke.

Trainer A device resembling a control or operating station, used to train operators.

Turn-and-bank indicator An aircraft instrument that shows the pilot the degree of bank and the rate of turn of the airplane.

Weightlessness The condition in flight where a body is apparently weightless relative to another because they are both unsupported and are "falling together" as they move. (Usually termed "apparent" weightlessness.)

INDEX

Italicized page numbers refer to illustrations.

.

ABOUT THE AUTHORS

Norman F. Smith worked for many years as an aerospace engineer and research scientist with NASA. He has written thirteen books on a wide range of scientific topics as well as numerous magazine and newspaper articles. He is also a pilot and served for four years in the Vermont House of Representatives. He lives in Vermont with his wife, Evelyn.

Douglas W. Smith, his son, is a pilot for a major airline and holds a master's degree in clinical psychology. He lives in Vermont with his wife, Dianna, and their three children.